Dedication:

To My Mom, Constance Fox-Bonomo. Thank you for teaching me the value of wisdom, reading, saving and teaching me to laugh like nobody is watching. All of my accomplishments are your legacy. You are always remembered and never forgotten. I love you.

INTRODUCTION ................................................................3

Planning for Advantage ........................................................5

THE FIRST TEN DAYS ................................................................10

THE NEXT TEN DAYS ................................................................33

THE FINAL TEN DAYS ................................................................51

The Final days and beyond: The Battle plan for repeatable
productivity ................................................................83

CONCLUSION................................................................87

# THE JANUARY ADVANTAGE METHOD

## J.A.M.

## INTRODUCTION

The January Advantage Method (J.A.M.) is my first endeavor to accumulate, organize and deconstruct a thirty day system to make progress every day on the important elements and values in one's life. Setting and achieving lifelong goals requires a combination of occasional, large leaps forward, but mostly, small, daily, steps makes up the majority of the journey. When this project was completed, a resource that other people could use to achieve the same ends had developed. A resource to assist motivated individuals to think through long-term projects and succeed in the consistent betterment of one's life. Only by deconstructing success to its basic elements, can a path become clear to continued and consistent daily progress. Finally, making that system straightforward and repeatable would ensure a proven method of exceeding potential. Using personal experiences and anecdotes was a vital part to any relatable narrative and as such I have included same here as well.

As an attorney and founding partner of my law firm, it becomes easy to forget the basic steps and strategies needed to become self-sufficient. This book is a realignment tool to get me, and you, back on track. A book which could be used by anybody starting their own career or business. A book that could help those stagnant in their careers to get back to basic and continuous progress. Creating value for those who have lost their way in the grind and put their dreams on hold, this book uses several anecdotes which I am most familiar with, such as legal strategies, negotiations and writing. The thirty steps I outline here are meant to be useable by anybody in any field or profession.

Most importantly, these are not time consuming tasks, just simple, powerful jump-starts you can implement on a daily basis to get going in the right direction.

Making progress every day is the only way to not only meet your goals consistently but also to make your dreams come true. The J.A.M. is a system that has worked for me and many of the attendees at my seminars and lectures. These thirty steps are a way to execute rather than theorize. Action steps rather than mere platitudes pushes the JAM forward. Each chapter includes writing cues to begin the JAM journal which is an integral part of the system but more on that later. So without further ado let's start the JAM.

## THE JANUARY ADVANTAGE METHOD (J.A.M.)

There is only one rule for success, "Make progress every day". The January Advantage Method is a system designed to plan, progress and complete tasks with consistent efficiency. Why January? The idea is simple. The first month of the year marks a new cycle in our lives. Similar to our birthday, January is a month of reflection and motivation to be better in the upcoming year. If you are a student you have the added benefit of September as also being a new year. Similarly, many industries have initial months which promise the same potential for rapid growth. All of these "starting points" January, birthdays, September, financial quarters are what I like to call personal/professional growth cycles. The JAM is designed to be implemented at the beginning of any and all of these cycles. These growth cycles are synonymous with "January" throughout this essay, and the purpose is to get you started whatever day of the year it is.

January inspires and motivates us to a degree that is rarely seen throughout the year. We envision our highest and best self and we are hopeful and inspired by the limitless potential of the year ahead. Unfortunately, three weeks later we have surrendered to the temptation and plodding realty of our lives. The ambition and motivation have flickered and been snuffed out. By February we have once again accepted the grim redundancy of mediocrity.

The solution is simple, harness and deconstruct the motivation and spirit of January and execute a plan to gain the advantage on a repeated basis.

## Planning for Advantage

*"It is never too late to be what you might have been"*- George Eliot

Before delving into the first month, the most important element of this method is that we recognize the advantage that is inherent in January. In fact, we must always be looking for upcoming advantages. What events are coming up this week that you have some sort of edge or advantage? What opportunities to learn will present themselves today? are you ready to focus during these crucial times? Have you set aside all distractions? Have you scheduled your three most important events and can these events receive your intense focus? By asking and answering these questions we can plan for daily advantages. By planning to maximize an advantage this week, we will begin the process of training ourselves to always be seeking out opportunity.

Some more focused questions to ask about the upcoming week are: Is there an upcoming networking event? can I spend an hour on getting my taxes/finances in order? Can I finally finish that book that's been laying on the couch for months? Ask these questions often and you will train your mind to watch for cues. Better yet create a JAM journal where you ask and answer these questions every day.

This search for an opportunity or advantage is what separates those who are good/average from those who are great and are looking forward to the week ahead. The difference between the good and the great is the different between comfortable, laid-back progress and savage, proactive hunger for success.

## **Two Approaches to completing long term tasks**

Once we are asking the questions that get us ready for the day and week ahead, it is also imperative that we begin long term planning. I am always cautious not to look to far ahead in the future when doing long term planning because I am aware that there are many unforeseen detours along the way. I try to keep my planning confined to three month intervals. I discuss the reasoning behind the number three later in this book, but for the time-being, focus on goals that can either be completed or significantly advanced within the next three months.

Accomplishing long-term tasks provides sustained success and builds self-confidence, perseverance and patience. Long-term tasks require two elements, (1) decision and (2) micro-actions. In order to progress decisiveness and small, consistent actions, we can choose to use a comfortable approach or a savage approach.

### Basic (Comfortable) Approach

*"Life begins at the end of your comfort zone."* - Neale Donald Walsch.

Writing a book is a good example of a long-term project requiring decisiveness and micro actions. A comfortable deadline for a first draft of a short book or novel would be one year. Using the comfortable approach, you can design your book-writing schedule around you other activities. Create a plan that fits comfortably around your more "important" tasks. After all, someone has to do the laundry, go food shopping and walk the dog. Daily chores, while necessary, trick us into thinking we are being productive. Soon becoming a published author gets pushed to a secondary priority, and passing on your ideas to the world becomes an unrealized dream.

In the comfortable approach you can decide to write a book, you can schedule blocks of time to work on the project and try your best to stick to it. You can brainstorm and write down notes on note cards. You can outline summaries, transitions and add clever anecdotes as you write. Soon you will develop a habit of only writing in perfect conditions and constantly revising as you write.

You can watch the days and weeks go by confident that creativity spurts are bound to happen soon. Deadlines will come and go and you will liberally grant yourself extensions without repercussions. Soon you will see your research grow stale and bemoan the fact as other authors write what you wanted to say. How many times have you had a great idea only to see it executed by someone else? Ideas are plentiful but action and execution are rare gems. Soon, in the comfortable approach, you will welcome the end of the year and the limited progress you have made vowing to begin again on January 1st. You will vaguely remember someone telling you that we are highly motivated in January and will patiently wait until then to begin. In January, you will come out of the gates strong as you start your second year of writing your book. You will create page after page of content. But at the end of the second year you will still not have the book. You will have good intentions and a great early effort but no product. The comfortable ultimately fails in its end goal.

Simply put, comfort is the enemy of progress, use this approach to pursue your goals and you will typically fail more than you succeed.

## Exceptional (Savage) Approach

*"Peace- it does not mean to be in a place where there is no challenge, no noise, no trouble or hard work. It means to be in the midst of all those things and still be calm in your heart."-* Unknown.

The other approach is the exceptional or savage approach to goal completion. You can approach a long term project such as writing a book like a battle. You can set a challenging deadline for yourself, such as 5-10 pages a week. The first draft to be completed in three months. A deadline with real-world consequences, such as depriving yourself of your favorite food (or perhaps any food) for a day. If you miss your deadline you must double your efforts in the subsequent sessions to catch up. You have a word limit to meet, and that is what matters most. You will brainstorm, write content and correct as you write. You will keep your notes organized and turn them into content every chance you get. You can write down anything you can think of to meet the deadline. Refine, revise and correct. And at the end of the year or sooner you will have completed something. Your first or perhaps final draft of something.

A product, a book, your goal, your dream. Then the real work begins…

After the initial draft you must not fear massive, edits and deletions. Seek honest criticism and proof your work no fewer than three read-through.

At this point in time I am supposed to say that the proper approach is somewhere in between the quality of comfortable writing and the quantity of savage writing, but it's not. Savagery is the correct approach. Be savage in your quest to complete your goal. Inevitably, you will refine your work, but that must come later. Writing a book is a challenge and they only way to get started is to actually write the first draft. Anything less is failure. The goal is to get published. The path can be planned, but you must act savagely. Save the comfortable approach for your later books.

Combine the two mindsets above, seek an advantage every day, and savagely pursue long term projects or dreams in three month intervals, and you will be ready to execute the J.A.M.

### J.A.M. Journal Writing Cues

**Begin your path to consistent progress and success today. Start a J.A.M. journal dedicated to daily achievement.**

**What three things can I do in my profession or career to move from my comfort zone and into a state of savage achievement?**

**1.**

**2.**

**3.**

**The Take Action Step** in the following pages we will suggest action steps and exercises for improving elements essential to the JAM. The first step is to create a J.A.M. Journal (pen and paper works best) in which you monitor times of the day when you are at your most energetic/productive and in a "flow state". Compare this to the times of day when you are tired and your willpower is depleted. This will allow you to create a reference point to return to, and focus on optimal times of the day in which to start new projects and gain momentum on important life goals.

This book is written to be a short manual aimed at getting you started today. The writing cues are there to provide reference points to harness your motivation and get back into a productive mindset.

The journal will also warn you when failure is likely. You will notice patterns in your writing and answering of the questions. Some answers will be productive and come from a motivated state whereas others will be cliché or redundant. Notice these writing patterns and learn when and where you are likely to succeed and when you are likely to enter into a slump. By learning what times of the day you are most likely to falter you can prepare small 5-10 minute counter measures which are discussed later in this book.

Success in all activities, especially in professional development, requires knowing when your willpower will be at optimum levels and maintaining momentum. Personally, I am an early riser. I prefer to get out of bed at the break of dawn and start planning. There are those who excel at late night momentum and creativity. Decide which method works best for you based on the journaling exercise in order to maximize your momentum.

The best way to use this book is to read it through completely in one or two sittings then revisit it and start creating the J.A.M. journal to monitor your productivity. So let's get started with the J.A.M.

*"If we all did the things we are capable of doing, we would literally astound ourselves"* - Thomas Edison

### Day 1  Never leave a project unimproved.

In the introduction, I stated that the one rule for success is to make progress every day. In order to do this, never leave an important project unimproved. This goes for everything you do in your life. Never walk out of a room without improving it somehow. Never leave your desk without a quick burst of organization for tomorrow.  Never close a computer file until you are sure you backed it up. Never check your email without deleting or organizing your subject folders. Never touch a book or file without reading and making notes in it. Do this for thirty days and massive progress is guaranteed.

To perform exceptionally, you must first convince yourself to savagely start a project, tirelessly improve it, develop a flexible plan as you progress and finally, relentlessly meet your self-imposed deadlines. Self-imposed deadlines occur well before actual real-world deadlines and allow you to think about a project and tweak it in the final days.  It is this final tweaking that often produces stellar results.  However, we cannot achieve this state of exceptional production until the foundation is complete and our mind is at rest.

This essay does not sugar-coat productivity. There is no one-size fits all when it comes to getting into a flow state. However, always improving a project is a guarantee to get you closer to flow state every day.

You must force yourself into discomfort, work through tiredness and believe that you can give one ounce more to a project. You must force yourself into social interactions. You must impose severe spending constraints and savings requirements for missed deadlines. You must assign an accountability partner to keep you on track. Assign penalties when you do not meet deadlines and never let a project go past six days with a review or re-organization. Keep track of the days you do not work on a project and your mind will force you to revisit it.  However, if you let seven days go by, your mind will convince you that there is nothing to be done or it can wait for later.

Am I really committed to this dream? Remember that dreams are what change your life, goals are the steps to get to dreams. Goals are fixed targets, they are good for getting us on track but they are bad for staying motivated. Don't be goal-oriented or results oriented. Rather be process oriented to achieve success.

**Action Step** - Always improve a project no matter how slight.

### J.A.M. Journal Writing Cue:

**What project or long term goal can I improve upon every day for the next thirty days which will significantly impact my reputation in my professional circle of friends and influence?**

**1.**

**What are some daily improvements on this project that I can implement this week?**

**A.**

**B.**

**C.**

### Day 2 - Understand that Willpower is a finite resource

Momentum is the fuel which drives success, however, our willpower is finite. In order to truly take advantage of the initial momentum inherent in "starting strong" we need to understand ourselves. Understanding when our willpower is depleted throughout the day is an essential element. In the book *Willpower by Tierny and Baumeister*, the authors describe willpower as a replenish-able source of energy. It ebbs and flows throughout the day and throughout the week. Each individual has unconsciously created a pattern for his/her willpower. This pattern can be adjusted to maximize productivity by scheduling important tasks for periods of strong focus. Furthermore, by eliminating temptations during periods of low willpower we can avoid or limit setbacks.

You must know yourself and your habits. You must execute difficult tasks at optimum intervals of high energy and willpower. Likewise, you must eliminate temptations and distractions during the time of day when your willpower is at its lowest. Make a plan to substitute bad habits such as late night eating with short intervals of willpower exercises i.e. before eating drink three glasses of cold water. Etc.

**Action Step** - Record times when your energy is highest and schedule the most difficult and time consuming tasks for those time periods.

### J.A.M. Journal Writing Cue:

**Based on the prior seven days, what times of the week was my willpower at its strongest?:**

**When was my will power at its lowest?:**

**Are there any specific interactions with people or places in which I am most likely to give in to temptations?**

## Day 3-Using the J.A.M. Journal to create effective processes oriented thinking.

The January Advantage Method requires one indispensable tool, a journal to plan and track progress. I have read dozens of books detailing the lives and habits of highly successful people and by far, the greatest habit they all have in common is journaling. In 2014 I conducted a self-experiment. This experiment led to a series of seminars, which led to an article, which led to the book you are reading today.

The January Advantage Method started as a journal I wrote to understand the extra boost of momentum all of us experience at the beginning of the New Year.

The question I wrote on the first page of the journal was simple, why are we Motivated in January? The Answer was life-changing for me. Now the question I write on the first day of the year is how can I duplicate the J.A.M. throughout the year?

All good experiments require a structured analysis. The journal I created focused on the three pillars of a good life as told to us by Benjamin Franklin. Health, wealth and wisdom/learning are the basic elements for success in life. So the first step in taking advantage of increased motivation is making these goals a priority in life. Setting weekly goals in this journal, recording productive and non-productive activities became the tools to measuring productivity.

I also created a self-scoring system of 1-10 which became imperative for graphing the data at the end of the 30 day exercise. I urge you to use a similar technique to quickly discover your strengths and identify your weakness. This J.A.M. Journal will set the baseline for your current level of motivation and every month thereafter will be compared to it. This step is indispensable.

On the first page of your JAM journal you will write down your major goals for the next thirty days. Next you will compile an action checklist. An action checklist is a list of at least ten items which you consider productive. These items will consist of short but powerful momentum builders, some examples are -

Read ten pages a day;

Spend ten minutes organizing the home office;

Use 10 minutes at the end of the day to eliminate and sort emails etc.

These action items are not complete tasks and you will only be allotting no more than ten minutes to the tasks. These incremental tasks should be linked to your thirty day goals that we write in the beginning of the JAM journal.

The list will likely evolve over the next thirty days as you become more focused and productive. You will begin to read faster and retain more information. You will be able to react quicker to emergencies and see your productivity soar. These ten minute improvements are called micro actions. Micro actions are at the heart of consistent daily progress. The more micro actions you remember to execute the faster massive projects will move forward.

**Action Step** - Record both your gains and success but also take detailed notes regarding your failures and set-backs. Note where you became sidetracked throughout the day and begin thinking about how to avoid these distractions in the future.

Grade each week on a scale of 1-10 in order to graph progress, recognize the pattern and plan the next week accordingly. Create an incremental checklist of at least 10 items with approximately 10 minutes allocated to each item.

## J.A.M. Journal Writing Cue:

**List five micro actions (10 minute productivity surges) that you can implement in your work and home life this week:**

    **1.**

    **2.**

**3.**

**4.**

**5.**

### Day 4- Dedicate time each week to the three pillars of a productive life, Health, Wealth and Wisdom.

When you first start your JAM journal you may wonder what topics to revisit each day. It is sometimes frustrating to think of something to write in your journal, especially if you had a very busy or hectic day.

Benjamin Franklin's golden rule "Early to bed early to rise keeps a man healthy wealthy and wise" provides us with three of the four pillars to a productive life. By asking ourselves what aspect Health, Wealth, Wisdom we have worked on provides us with a starting point for our daily entry. The final pillar is happiness.

**Health** - Every January gym memberships and diet supplements sales skyrocket. Everyone becomes health conscious in the beginning of the year. Use this social momentum to your advantage. Set a sustainable goal and process to achieve it. Because of the spike in interest in healthy living you will likely be exposed to increased healthy advertisements, and articles about healthy living. It's impossible to know if the increased attention by outside forces is a causation element or a correlation element of our increased motivation, but this added attention to healthy living can be channeled into productivity. Take advantage of the gym membership discounts and hit the crowded gyms.

Most of the crowds along with the social motivation will dissipate by February 1, 2016. Therefore, as the gym becomes less crowded continue to increase your dedication to a healthy lifestyle and stick to the schedule you set previously.

When you go to the Gym in January, be confident in the knowledge that you have a plan to keep this healthy lifestyle the entire year. Most people will give up by February 1st anyway so you might as well exhaust yourself along with all the rest, and keep the momentum going into the second month to develop a habit of healthy living. Unlike those who will quit, you have the JAM to keep the momentum.

**Wisdom** - Similarly, set a challenging goal for self-education. You must set aside time daily and weekly to learn something new and hone the skills you already have. For example, select the five books you must read this year and attack them ferociously. Set a daily reading goal and a weekly goal to stay on target. Submit to early "motivation surge" that comes with writing down a daily and weekly plan with challenging goals. Unlike the others who will trail off by February or sooner, be confident that you have a plan to keeps this going the entire year. By developing a system of goal achievement you are guaranteed to outlast those who simply "wish to read more this year".

Try to read one book a week instead of one a month. Set challenging goals early in the JAM, but unlike the others who fail by February, you will develop a system of goal achievement in this most crucial element of your life. The Pursuit of knowledge should never be abandoned when you finish school, on the contrary the end of formal education is simply the beginning of the true knowledge-building that awaits us.

**Wealth** - The third pillar of a productive life is wealth and career building. Set your wealth goals and career goals for the month. Get ahead at work and stay ahead. Do all the little tasks that "clear the decks" and get organized. If you can go in on the weekends leading up to the beginning of the JAM then plan to do it. Using off-hours to set up your day is an excellent strategy to getting ahead and staying productive. Be confident in knowing that this extra effort now will clear the way for productivity throughout the year.

Start you incremental checklist and place copies of it wherever you will be throughout the day. One thing I learned very quickly when I started implementing the JAM is the idea that I need to have my reminders everywhere. I soon learned that confining my thoughts to one journal or having one quiet place to review my goals would never work. When you write your to do list, take pics of it with your phone. Photocopy it at the office. Place an extra copy in your car. This process of redundant reminders will improve your memory and scheduling skills exponentially.

Make multiple of important tasks and notes, and attach notes and files to digital calendar events. At home I work on a dry erase board and I usually snap a picture of it before I leave for the day, doing this leaves me with no guilty feelings when I wipe it clean the next day and write a new set of ideas down. I also snap a picture of the wall calendar at work before leaving. Always keep copies of your goals in your car, workplace and home. Always discard papers and notes when they are accomplished or dated. Do not become attached to information you created simply because you created it. This will lead to a hording situation. Become an efficient organizer by purging weekly or biweekly.

The incremental checklist contains micro actions structured to keep you on task. This flexible list must always be nearby. The incremental checklist is the list which you will always have with you through those inevitable slumps in productivity.

Redundancy is also the key to keep journaling every day. One frequent complaint I hear about journaling is that people start strong but then peter off as the months go by. Sounds familiar right? Many people will go out and buy a nice journal and select a spot where they love to write in that journal. Then as the reality of life sets in and the journal gets misplaced or destroyed the motivation wanes. When the writer cannot get to their favorite spot the journal sits closed. Do not become tied to the physical journal. You will lose it and it will contain many cringe-inducing thoughts which you may never want to review. The more important point is keep writing. Write in multiple locations and in several journals. Redundancy will keep you writing when others have given up.

One of the best writing tips I ever heard was to write for the waste bin first and foremost. Get your thoughts out and organized. Do not be afraid to write content that is destined for the trash. Free yourself to write by doing this. This experiment is probably the greatest one you will ever implement as you will be testing and extending your potential, so commit to the next thirty days and watch your productivity amaze even yourself.

**Action Step-** Set up your three or more goals that you want to accomplish this month. Typically they will fit within one of three categories Health, Wealth and Wisdom/learning. Embrace the added energy and positivity of the JAM and begin implementing your incremental checklist of micro actions and make it redundant.

### J.A.M. Journal Writing Cue:

**Health - What three things can I do to improve my health this month?**

A.     **Exercise -**

B.     **Diet/Nutrition-**

C.     **Sports and Social Activities -**

**Wealth - What things can I do to improve my wealth this month?**

A.     **Improve skill set**

B.     **Saving and investing**

**Wisdom - What can I do to continue learning every day?**

**<u>Day 5 - Get Organized and Dominate the Competition</u>** - Implementing a "sleep-work-reflect" triad into your schedule is vital to success. I am extremely biased towards rising early as a way to dominate the competition. However, the true secret to doing better than your competitors is to be organized earlier. There is a magic in the quiet, early morning hours that allows one to get prepared for the day. There is no rush to get things done. There is a natural relaxed atmosphere that allows for early planning.

I limit what I eat in the morning. This was very difficult for me because I love to eat and I love breakfast. But once I reduce my morning meal, my energy level in the early morning became increased significantly. I still let myself indulge in big breakfasts on Saturday and Sunday.

The benefits of being a morning person are self-evident and rewarding. Arriving early gives me an advantage over other attorneys who are rushing to get into the Court or to their meetings. Getting to the office early allows me to ease into big projects and knock out small projects. There is a natural confidence and pride I feel when I know that I have completed a project, motion, essay or brief before my adversary has even gotten out of bed. I have taught by example and have had many associates tell me how their "luck" changed for the better when they get to Court early or get a project done ahead of time. This concept of luck is more of a result of appearing prepared rather than a fortuitous event.

Getting organized earlier allows more time for the subconscious to tweak your work as you work on other mundane or routine tasks. This cooling off period is vital to authors, students and all professionals who write. By finishing early you maximize the creativity that is generated during the reflection period.

Contrast this to someone who likes to write at night before going to bed. The subconscious reflection period now takes place in the form of dreams, when you can take little action except try to remember them when you wake up. The early riser has the reflection or "ah ha" moment with pen and paper nearby. This is a great momentum builder.

Schedule your creative projects as early as possible. For the reasons set forth above, do your writing before your routine tasks. If you have mundane tasks schedule them for "second morning" (9:00 a.m. to 11:30 a.m.) or later. Make "First morning" (5:30 a.m. to 8:30am) your time to progress your dreams. The benefit of harnessing your subconscious throughout the day is your most valuable asset.

**Action Step** - Commit to dominating the day by maximizing the hours in which your competition is probably neglecting. Whenever you wake up review your JAM journal and get organized. Be eager and energetic when you get out of bed in the morning and think of all the work your competitor is not getting done while they sleep and you grind.

**Time Saving Tip**- Early risers also see the benefit of getting up sooner on the weekend as well. Plan your weekends for "vigorous leisure", be active and energetic and make activity a synonym for relaxing as opposed to an opposite. Dominate the weekends like you dominate the competition.

**J.A.M. Journal Writing Cue:**

**If you could wake up two hours earlier than normal tomorrow write down three things you could get accomplished before the competition has even gotten out of bed.**

**1.**

**2.**

**3.**

### Day 6- That which is measured improves.  Use timers to stay on task.

Making progress everyday means, getting to what's most important to you on a daily basis.  Using a stop watch keeps you on task, allows you to take short breaks, and gets you back on task like no other tool.  Using a timer will get you on task on a daily basis and will keep you on task longer than a vague schedule or to do item.

Setting a ten minute timer to work on a project will help you avoid distractions.  Best of all, if you must take a break or an emergency occurs, you can stop the watch and restart it when you return to guarantee ten minutes of work on the project. The ability to stop the watch allows you to take a break, without detracting from the task at hand.

If you have allotted 1 hour of writing/reading time, and you take a ten minute break at the thirty minute mark, stop the watch so as not to lose the ten minutes from the overall tasks.  Do this one simple task for seven days and record your productivity.

The added benefit of using a timer is often realized in those final five minutes.  Time and time again, when I implement the timer technique, I will look down at the watch and see there is only five minutes left.  The mind shift that takes place is incredible.  When I started the project, I was so bored/frustrated that wished the timer would hurry up and hit the sixty minute mark so I could be done. However, as it neared the end, and I glanced down sudden desperate motivation would kick in and I frequently wrote 10-20% of the content in that last five minute session.  Typically, I go over the hour on a project that I was dreading and which I had plodded through for the first fifty-five minutes.

**Action Step** Invest in a dedicated stop watch (not the phone or computer) to time your tasks.  Take guilt free breaks knowing that you can't end until you have worked the allocated amount of time on the project. Record the progress gained in the final five minutes of the timed task and write down how you felt when you were forced to be "in the zone".  This is the element we are trying to recreate as often as possible in the JAM.

## J.A.M. Journal Writing Cue:

**What project (s) can you work on this week using a timer to stay on task and make daily progress with?**

**1.**

**2.**

**3.**

## Day 7- Start a Daily Savings Plan

Saving money on a daily basis no matter how little or how much is an absolute must to getting an advantage and being productive. Saving as little as three dollars a day for the next thirty days will not only be an excellent metric to track your progress with JAM. Daily saving will build and strengthen the most important habit -Discipline. At first this appears to be nothing more than simple, sound, economic advice, however I have discovered a significant psychological advantage inherent in daily savings plans.

I have been saving money every day for over ten years. When I say "saving" I mean physically taking the money out of my stream of income and expenses and putting it in a secure setting. This is different from savings money in banks, and other investments.

At times it was challenging scrapping together a few dollars to save and at times it has been liberating, saving hundreds of dollars in a single day. You must understand that daily saving requires physically taking money out of your wallet (purse, pocket etc.) and placing it in a separate savings container. The amount of money saved at the end of the thirty day JAM is irrelevant.

This discipline of daily progress is what matters. When you create a habit of saving money every day, your mind does not rest easy until you have completed this activity. Once done, your mental checklist is satisfied and you can complete your day. The added benefit is obvious, your personal disposable income grows over time, which increases your overall confidence and motivates you to be more disciplined with money. It is the perfect good habit cycle that we seek to recreate every day with the JAM.

**Action Step**- set a modest daily savings goal. You must physically remove $2.00 or $3.00 dollars from your wallet and place it into a savings container and out of your stream of income.

**J.A.M. Journal Writing Cue:**

**Set down a modest daily savings plan for the next six months. Create a base number, a small as possible, but commit to saving that amount of money every day. Write down your savings goal for the year. List three daily expenses you can reduce or eliminate to help guarantee a daily savings habit, such as bring lunch to work instead of eating out etc.:**

**1.**

**2.**

**3.**

## Day 8- The Golden Rule Of Three

*"Live by the trinity of what is true, good and beautiful."*- Alexandra Stoddard.

*"Early to bed, early to rise, makes a man healthy, wealthy and wise."* - Benjamin Franklin

In the book, The Presentation Secrets of Steve Job, author Carmine Gallo describes the power of three. Steve Job perfected an approach of deconstructing complex into elegant and simple designs. The master of making technology simple beautiful and functional (notice the three elements) he endeavored and succeeded in keeping his product, presentation and marketing focused on the three major elements of new technology that his company produces.

Utilizing, what Jobs refers to as "the magic power of three". The rule of three states that in any presentation to an audience we should endeavor to deconstruct the material into three (or fewer) main elements. Audiences have very short attention spans and you want to limit most presentations to thirty minutes or less, convey three main points or less in that time and maximize your time by forcing the focus. Tight presentation time constraints and simple three part structures produced staggering profits for Apple.

This power of three is evident in every effective writing, debate, and presentation. Aside from audience interest, the other valuable aspect of the power of three is that it makes the author narrow his/her focus to three elements which then forces the author to explain these elements as fully and succinctly as possible.

Multiples of three are also all around us. J.A.M. is a method based on thirty interchangeable rules for thirty days towards increased productivity. Ben Franklin chose three pillars of living a productive life and you should endeavor to implement the rule of three in your projects as well.

**Action Step** - Utilize the power of three in your everyday projects. Implement three in how you set your goals. Schedule your day into three sections every day. Select three books you want to read during the next thirty days and schedule time to complete the task. In the next daily tip I will share my private algorithm which I utilize to get started on difficult projects and stay motivated to finish.

**J.A.M. Journal Writing Cue:**

**List the three major tasks/projects that make up the majority of your work day:**

1.


2.

**3.**

      What can you do to improve upon executing and accomplishing these three major tasks on a daily basis? List three or more ideas for improving efficiency in these major tasks:

**1.**



**2.**



**3.**


## Day 9 - The Paradox of Choice.  Where to start? Develop an algorithm for your profession .The Rule of 1-3-5 and the Rule of 3-5-10.

*"When making a decision of minor importance I have always found it advantageous to consider all pros and cons as they teach us in school.*

*In vital matters however, the decision should come from the unconscious (the gut) somewhere within ourselves.*

*In the important decisions of personal life and relationships we should be governed by the deepest, inner needs of our nature and values." -* Sigmund Freud.

      The paradox of choice states that choice is an illusion of freedom.  We perceive having choices as having freedom, when in fact too much variety is often paralyzing and results in inaction more often than not.

The January Advantage Method seeks to create momentum and narrow the focus to basic, simple, powerful forward moving tasks. The quicker we start a task, the quicker we finish. The more tasks we complete the more productive we become. The more productive we become the more value we have to ourselves, family and work. In order to develop momentum in my professional career I created two sets of numbers, which were easy to remember and which could act as a trigger to my creative process. While not technically an algorithm, the first series of number is my Goal Setters Rule.

<u>1-3-5 The Goal Setter Rule</u>

One- Set one major goal for the day. A Major goal will usually take dozens of hours to complete over the course of weeks or months. The JAM will teach you how to accomplish these tasks in half the time. The one major goal is the thing you most want to accomplish today, it should be challenging and significant to your progress and success. This Major goal should be placed in your schedule with at least one hour work using a timer to stay on task. ( I talk about timing strategies earlier in this book) This block should be scheduled as early as possible. Dr. Stephen Covey refers to these tasks as the Important-Not Urgent Task. It is a task which will be a proactive task making your future goals attainable.

Three- Set three mid-range goals to attempt today. These are your urgent items that need to get done today and which are required for your continued success and progress but can be accomplished, or at least progressed, in a block of forty-five minutes or less. You will try to make progress on all three of these tasks in a relatively short amount of time. Dr. Covey describes these tasks as Urgent and Important. The bulk of our day usually contains these items but it is our duty to control the impact of these items so we can work on improving our future.

Five- Finally, Set five mundane/routine tasks, chores and necessary activities. These can be tasks such as responding to emails, voicemail, file management and follow up memos. This is a good block of time to allocate to unexpected events and duties that may arise throughout the day. Try to save your urgent tasks for this allocated block of time rather than letting these tasks detract from the important goal progression of the one and three goals. You should set a block of time of about thirty minutes to complete these tasks near the end of the day preferably. Keep 1-3-5 in mind all day. Dr. Covey refers to these tasks as urgent but not important tasks.

Once you goals have been set, the daunting question of "where to begin?" surfaces. It's easy to write down your major and intermediate goals, but how exactly do you delve into that box of papers, computer files and/or pictures to get the project started? To respond to this question, I created the second series of numbers:

### 3-5-10 the Task Starter Rule

Rule 3-5-10 is what I call my task-starter rule. The task starter rules breaks down any challenging task into a numeric pattern. This rule has been foolproof in getting me to roll up my sleeves and tackle the most difficult cases in my firm with a tremendous success rate.

I would like to take a moment and address a question that you may have raised at this point. Specifically, these sets of numbers seem to be just an arbitrary selection and connected to any established pattern. The truth of the matter is that our brains are not statistical machines. Arbitrary motivation is more effective than calculations and scientific foundation. This is why anecdote is more memorable than statistics. We are simply wired in a way to remember simple sets of numbers rather than complex calculations.

That having been said, whenever someone tells you of foolproof way to achieve your goals, you owe it to yourself to try it at least once and record your own conclusions.

Three - As I stated earlier, any project, no matter how complex, has three major elements. It is our job to deconstruct the project into its three major components. If you cannot readily identify the three components of a project ask yourself, "what questions does the project seek to answer?"

I use the rule of three to get unstuck on difficult memos of law, briefs or other project in the office. I ask myself what is the goal

27

of this memo or letter? What three elements do I want to get across to the (judge, adversary, client etc.?)

I often remind myself of the rule of three by drawing a triangle and putting the most important element at the top. This small doodle activates a creative part of my brain and I can make connections that are not apparent on a linear line of text.

A listener who remembers what you said very often becomes a customer. Studies also show that clients and customers greatly appreciate simplicity and will not retain more than three things that you tell them at a meeting.

Five - After I have consolidated my data under three major headlines, the next step is to get external references to support these main points. Data-mining, in excess, (extensive online and book research) on the internet and in the library is a dangerous thing. We collect mountains of information but ultimately fail in the implementation of converting that data into useable results. In the beginning of a project I try to limit my supporting material to five articles of external support. This early narrowing of my sources forces me to be decisive early. As long as you start a project early, there will always be flexibility as the project progresses.

The myth of "working well under pressure" is often an excuse to put off work until the last minute, however it does have some credibility. Simply put, impending deadlines force creativity precisely because of the time constraint and the inability to submit to distraction. Therefore, setting multiple deadlines will trigger more creative solutions. The truth is time constraints forced us to be decisive. When you start a project on time and are decisive from the beginning, you are guaranteed to develop a stronger, more complete end-result every single time. Understanding how procrastination works, teaches us to get into the "flow state" more often.

Ten- I attended a lecture given by a professor from Stanford. He stated that nearly all tasks in your profession can be reduced and solved with ten (and often less)frequently used resources or skills you already have. He recommended clearing your desktop on your computer and selecting the ten most frequent letters/templates/files.

Reducing these icons on your screen to ten or less provides a task clarity state. Again you might be wondering why ten and not eight, and the answer which I provided earlier is that ten is an easy round number to remember. Our minds work well with anecdotes.

He states further to select the 10 frequently used manuals or books relevant to your profession and study those the most. The rule of ten in my series stands for using one or more of the ten frequently accessed resources and skills to progress a task. In summary, become an expert in the most frequent ten procedures that your company does and that expertise will solve Ninety percent of your problems at work.

**Action Step-** Develop a simple algorithm/series of numbers to activate you and trigger your goal strategy. Integrate the magic number three into your customized equation and get started on your strategy today.

**J.A.M. Journal Writing Cue:**

**Make a list of the ten most frequent resources, manuals, files used in your profession.**

1.                    2.                    3.



4.                    5.                    6.



7.                    8.                    9.



10.

**Day 10- Plan to be in full control of your work week by Wednesday.**

As you work through the second week of the J.A.M., make time to reflect on your progress. Review your J.A.M. journal and double down on the suggestions that resulted in increased daily activity. You should see that the above tools are working in conjunction with your highly motivated state.

It's important that you reflect on the progress you made and detail areas that need improvement. The rules are interchangeable, they are to be implemented in accordance with your time and energy levels. Some require more time than others but all of them are geared toward incremental micro-actions.

Remember that the ideal week, just like the JAM, starts with high levels of motivation and energy which depletes throughout the week. As you learn to self-motivate, you will learn to love Mondays and doubt those who complain about the first day of the work week.

Starting the week with a depressed attitude practically guarantees failure. On the contrary, look forward to Monday and schedule your most difficult and time consuming tasks for Monday to dominate the competition and gain an advantage.

Don't just plan for the day or week ahead rather have the next ten days roughly sketched out on Monday. Deadlines are your friend, use them to generate creativity and solutions. Be aware early of major events and meetings which are scheduled. My goal every Monday is the same, I want to be done with the heavy work no later than 12:30 Wednesday. I schedule the most time consuming tasks for as early on Monday as possible and try to work through with high energy.

While I don't always succeed getting the work week by Wednesday, this proactive approach always opens up great opportunities for the second half of the week.

I am able to be more flexible with my schedule in the latter half of the week. I can adapt and reschedule meetings which are convenient for all involved, and I can reflect on the work already completed. Short term reflection and improvement is what makes average work good, and good projects great.

## ACTION STEP

Starting Monday, like starting the JAM, requires a positive attitude. Grade your next work week on a scale of 1-10 with ten being optimal productivity and one being a potato. An ideal work week would look something like this:

Monday (energy level 10 or 9.5) - Tackling difficult tasks, completing and executing multiple mid-range tasks, and nearly all mundane tasks accomplished before the end of the work day.

Tuesday - (energy level 9.5 or 8.5) - Progressing difficult tasks, completing and executing mid-level tasks. Minimal time spent on mundane tasks.

Wednesday (energy level 8) - This should be your control day. By Wednesday you should have control over all tasks and be able to deal with urgent matters and emergencies with ease. You are ahead of schedule or at least on schedule with difficult long term tasks and you are already scheduling appointments for next week.

Thursday - (energy level 7) - Having gained control of your time and increased productivity allow for greater client-customer interaction and building networks. Advertising and improving your brand. Task completion is at an all-time high and tasks require minimal adjustment and micro improvements to stay on target.

Friday (energy level 7.5- 6) the vast majority of people will be panicking to get things done by Friday. Unlike you, many people will realize how little they got done throughout the week. Use this day to further connect with clients and build your brand. This strategy is optimal for my increased work flow and productivity.

## J.A.M. Journal Writing Cue:

**List three major tasks which can be substantially advanced on Monday and have a significant impact or reducing work load by Wednesday.**

1.

2.

3.

# THE NEXT TEN DAYS

*"Go confidently in the direction of your dreams! Live the life you've imagined."* - Thoreau

## Day 11- Develop good habits and smashing bad ones.

It takes 21 days to build a good habit. It takes about 30 days of concerted effort to eliminate bad habits. It also takes a lot more will power to smash bad habits. Bad habits are indulgences that continue far too long. One piece of dark chocolate is an adequate reward, eating a whole box of chocolates in one sitting is a destructive/bad habit. Watching You Tube/Netflix for a short amount of time is a leisurely indulgence. Binging on content for hours is a bad habit.

In the book The Power of Habit- Why we do what we do in life and Business, by Charles Duhigg, the author describes three elements of the bad habit loop: Cue- Routine- Reward.

Cue- is a location, event, time or place. It could be an advertisement or commercial with a delicious looking lasagna or coming home after a hard day of work and kicking off your shoes. This is a signal to the brain that it's time to trigger a bad habit, such as eating excessively, watching Netflix/YouTube and skipping exercise etc.

Routine- After the cue the bodily automatically activates the routine. This is the bad habit. The routine could be walking to the refrigerator, opening the bag of chips, ordering the pizza, crashing on the couch and grabbing the remote etc. It is the routine that it is automatic. The body can accomplish this without thinking. It is a habit reflex.

Reward- The body is rewarded with the immediate reward or stimulus, in the above example, overeating, finish an entire series of The Walking Dead, avoiding exercise.

In order to break the habit we don't have to change the cue, because we can't, nor the reward (however we can delay it). We need to examine and adjust the routine.

Identify the Cue - Coming home from work tired and kicking off your shoes. Identify the reward overeating, eating junk food. Then identify the routine- going to the refrigerator or ordering pizza. The solution is to delay the routine. Do whatever you can think of to delay the routine, a fifteen minute walk/jog on the tread mill, go for a walk, challenge yourself to drink a whole liter of water, read 10-20 pages.

This delay creates is known as a pattern interrupt. After the pattern interrupt, rate yourself, on a scale of 1-10 with 10 being an effective pattern interrupt and 1 being no change in the desire to indulge. Ask yourself, how bad do I still want the reward (eating/Netflix etc.)? If your answer is strong then the adjustment is not adequate to break the habit. Once you find a routine that reduces your craving for the reward then you are on the right track. In the future, every time you trigger the cue, activate the effective pattern interrupt before indulging in the reward. You will reduce the craving for the reward and break the bad habit cycle.

## ACTION STEP

Focus on building two to three good habits to replace the bad habits. Always record how you feel when a good habit replaces one of your bad habits. By distracting yourself from your bad habits you think about it less because you are focusing on the productive process. This will allow you to crush the bad habit when you decide it's time to eliminate it completely.

### J.A.M. Journal Writing Cue:

**List three bad habits that are keeping you from excelling in Health, Wealth and Wisdom. Apply the pattern interrupt to these habits over the next thirty days and record your progress.**

1.

2.

**3.**

### Day 12 Develop your strengths and focus on improving them.

*"Always dream and shoot higher than you know you can do. Don't bother just to be better than your contemporaries or predecessors. Try to be better than yourself."* - William Faulkner.

The strategies in the J.A.M. provide a framework obtain an edge over the competition and always be improving your strengths. It I better to be good at several complementary skills than great at one esoteric talent. This book has been focused on the advantage of January. The idea of "starting fresh" motivates us with a sense of achievement. When we combine that motivation with improving skills we will constantly outperform those even when others have inherent "natural" skill.

If your strength lies in client/customer interaction, then try to schedule additional time to interact with your clients/customers. Research social psychology and improve your presentation skills. Likewise, if you strong skill set lie in technology, increase your understanding of the tech field by attending conferences and engaging in like-minded networks. Simply put:

Improve your skill set = Increase in your value and income.

If you are a slow reader but really enjoy science fiction, consume double the amount of sci-fi books and material you normally read in a thirty-day period. Find your edge and improve upon it early.

Every morning when you are updating your J.A.M. journal, make it a habit to write down "how will I improve myself and my value today?" At the end of the day, record your successes in this area. Seek to obtain an advantage or edge in all tasks that you perform.

**Action Step**- Every morning, ask yourself "What is my strongest profession related skill? What can I do today to strengthen and improve that skill?" What one activity do you do at work that generates money for you or your company? How can you improve your performance in this task? Execute a plan to maximize your strength.

## J.A.M. Journal Writing Cue:

**How can you improve your major skill set(s) this week? List any upcoming conferences in your field of interest and enroll.**

**Upcoming lectures or conferences that will increase my understanding of** _____

1.


2.


3.


## Day 13 Incremental progress every day. One is greater than Zero (1>0)

"One is greater than Zero (1>0)" is the single most important rule for daily progression. Jot this down and place it somewhere to remind you of this obvious but powerful trigger. This is one of those simple rules that needs to be repeated and drilled into our brains every chance we get. Write this simple formula at the top of those projects that just refuse to get started.

This concept is optimal to use on those projects that are intimidating and avoided at all costs.

Every difficult project, from the pyramids to the founding of the United States begins with an incremental step forward. When you don't know where to start, take a pen and paper and start writing a summary of what needs to be accomplished on a certain project. Simply doing something, triggers a problem-solving mentality in all of us.

Thinking about a problem is not doing something. It is necessary to think about a problem, but the mind is too dynamic and prone to wander, it needs constraints. If starting a project is too difficult, then take a pen and paper and simply write down what obstacles are making the project stagnate. Get into the habit of creating a foolproof problem solving mechanism. Create a paradigm in which the solution must begin to manifest. Execution of simple tasks makes it easier to deconstruct larger projects into their components.

One sentence written on paper is typically more important than hours of thought and pondering on a problem, because the writing is an implementation step. Typically, the physical act of writing a summary of the issues leads to the writing down of possible solutions. The process of selecting words means that you are simultaneously eliminating millions of other words and that's how solutions are born. Begin and do something

Some examples of One is greater than Zero:

If you want to do 100 pushups do 1.

If you want to write a 200 page novel, write one sentence.

If you want to lose weight make your decision to eat healthy at the next meal.

Incremental progress + dedication = massive success in the long term.

**Action Step**- Locate those projects that have been sitting around gathering dust. Take out a clean sheet of paper and write this simple equation at the top of the sheet $1>0$. Ask yourself what is the smallest possible thing I could do to get this project started. For example can I organize the papers into chronological order? Write the contacts number on the front of the file, should I call a contact person for more information? Simply dedicate one minute to completing this tiny task.

**J.A.M. Journal Writing Cue:**

**Begin a difficult project today. Write down three basic steps that could be done in a few minutes or less that would start this project moving forward. Execute at least one step forward today.**

**1.**

**2.**

**3.**

## Day 14 When we take action we are building courage.

*"Courage does not always roar. Sometimes courage is the quiet voice at the end of the day saying, I will try again tomorrow."* - Mary Ann Radmacher.

*"Do something today, anything, which the world may talk of hereafter"* - Alexander the Great.

Alexander the Great conquered the world and was known by all as a general who took action twice as much as any other. It is no surprise that men and women of action are often considered brave, innovative and bold. Action and courage are synonyms in our professional lives as well. All success stories have these three elements, 1. Action- swift and decisive decisions to perform a task to the best of one's ability; 2. Courage to attempt something without caring what others will think, to put aside intimidation and be confident that you have prepared sufficiently for the moment; 3.Repeat step one and two, there is no third element.

Courage to act in all endeavors invariably leads to success. This is true in education, in work, in the law and in all social interactions. When you are reluctant to act, or when action seems improbable or unlikely, ask yourself, are you brave or a coward? If you want to think of yourself as brave, than act now. Implement any step no matter how small that will move you closer to your goal.

**Action Step** - Substitute action for courage. Be brave and not fearful. A life is meant to be lived. Taking action and being brave are the critical elements to a courageous life. Let the average people be timid and reserved. Let us act with bravery strength and decisive action. Commit to action today.

### J.A.M. Journal Writing Cue:

**Do not think of your projects or career in terms of mundane statistics and to do lists. Rather think of your tasks as being completed decisively and with courage, or avoided as a coward would avoid a battle.**

**List several tasks that can be approached with this mindset of courage and complete them relentlessly:**

1.

2.

3.

4.

5.

### Day 15 Don't just set goals, create your own "System for Success".

The J.A.M. is my system for success. It works for me and hopefully some of these tips will work for you. You owe it to yourself to create a system that works for you. It needs to be repeatable and last for thirty days or more.

Throughout the year I am asked to speak on a variety of subjects. One series of lecturers I gave is dedicated to helping others become successful, productive entrepreneurs. I always start the series with a discussion of goals vs. systems.

Following is an excerpt from one such presentation:

I want to talk about Goals. What most of you think of as goals are not goals but results. You might write down that your professional goal for this month is to obtain ten new customers or clients. Then you will write down a plan to obtain these customers using elements such as lead generation, cold calling, follow up and other various techniques to turn a prospect into a client/customer. At the end of the month you will have either obtained ten new customers or more than likely failed to meet this goal.

The number of client conversions at the end of the month is not a good goal. It is actually a result. The goal in the above example should be to develop a repeatable prospect to conversion plan. Your goal for the month might be to implement an effective customer outreach plan. This goal can never be achieved, rather it will evolve into other greater goals.

If your system of goal attainment yields the results you want, i.e. ten new clients in a month, then you will ask yourself how do I "scale" this plan upwards to create twenty new clients a month? You may require additional employees, or you may decide to focus on other resources like advertising. Your system may then evolve to develop a marketing plan. Successful people always talk about scaling a product, procedure or service. You must always be thinking about scaling your system upward. In the above example your new goal will evolve into increased conversions or possibly a marketing plan. Your result, i.e. 20 new clients is not the goal, rather you have developed a system or client conversion plan.

If you don't achieve a certain goal/result this leads to discouragement. People who are result oriented tend to abandon ideas and systems when the results are not what they expect. However, the best way to constantly achieve goals is to utilize a system. System oriented people understand this and they stay with ideas that work and complete more projects.

You will often miss the mark in a results-oriented mindset and often the reasons may be beyond your control. One month may be particularly bad because of weather, the economy or taxes. If you are result-oriented you way draw a conclusion that your plan to obtain clients has failed. This assumption may make you abandon an otherwise workable goal-achievement system.

Another way to summarize this is to be method-oriented rather than results-oriented. Results are vital to keep score, but methods are controllable experiments which can be tested and proven over time. Analyze and scale the method and the results will follow.

One common question I get asked by young entrepreneurs is how do I achieve certain monetary goals? i.e.

Goal- I want to make an extra $5,000.00 per year.

The amount of variables inherent in this goal makes it difficult to gauge this result. Furthermore, why limit the goal to $5,000 as opposed to $100,000.00. A better Goal would be:

I will make twenty extra calls to clients this month every day and record the results and effectiveness of this extra effort. The system of selecting a method to create sales rather than trying any possible sales generating activity is a plan that has long term potential.

There will always be some variables, but this system is much closer to being within one's own control. Either you made the calls or you didn't. The percent of conversions from calls can be recorded and scaled accordingly.

**Action Step** - Spend more time writing out your systems. Don't just write down results. Start with the result you want and work backwards. Ask yourself, what will it take to get to this result in a realistic time frame? Create "Goals" which look like methods rather than results, but use the results to gauge and analyze the methods. Once you have created a method that is nearly completely within your control (i.e. call ten new prospects every week) then make the method your goal and the results your scorecard.

### J.A.M. Journal Writing Cue

**Instead of writing down goal/results, make a list of three important systems you can use to attain those results. Work back from the results themselves and create systems for goal attainment:**

**1.**

**2.**

**3.**

### Day 16 Avoid the Nostalgia trap

*"Fame is a vapor, popularity an accident, riches take wings, only one thing endures and that is Character."* - Horace Greeley.

Nostalgia is big business. Just look at the current movies in theaters today. How many are sequels, remakes, prequels or old TV show derivatives? In the summer of 2016 Pokémon Go became the most downloaded app in 24 hours; this brand goes back to the early 90's.

Nostalgia is inherently deceptive. Our minds cherry pick the good and forget the bad. We, as a species, love to remember the past fondly. As an experiment, revisit the shows you watched when you were in high school. Odds are they will be slow, boring and filled with plot holes and not nearly as interesting as you remember.

Compare movies and music of your youth to modern media. The difference is not just cultural. Both the old and the new are far from perfect. They both have huge weaknesses.

The past is an important teacher and reminder to avoid failures and harm. However, it can also be a trap which leads us to dwell in a state of inaction and non-progression when used in our professional development.

Nostalgia tricks us every day into thinking that yesterday was better than today and probably better than the future. However, the opposite is true. The present is within our control and the future is filled with possibilities and opportunities. It is the past that cannot be improved, changed or otherwise acted upon. Fond memories are needed for comfort in our old age. But the only thing that it offers us today is a deep distraction to be avoided as much as possible.

**Action Step** - Nostalgia is big business and can be used to tug at the hearts and minds of potential customers. More often than not, it tricks us into being un-productive and longing for the old days. Limit your mental time travel as much as possible and focus on changing the limitless future to coincide with your own personal design. There's plenty of time for fond memories when we can no longer move quick and be decisive. Seize today and leave yesterday on Facebook and in photo albums.

### J.A.M. Journal Writing Cues

**Write down ways in which nostalgia has made you think that the past was better than the present. Compare the resources that are currently available and the time management techniques which have improved over the past decade.**

## Day 17 - Getting Unstuck -

Slumps, slowdowns and getting stuck is inevitable. No matter how productive we hope to be at the beginning of a week we will inevitably encounter unforeseen emergencies and energy drains. Eventually we all get stuck. Fortunately, there are several simple ways to dealing with the inevitable slow down:

1.    Allow yourself to be stuck for a while.  If you feel drained, tired, and otherwise unable to make any progress in the day, one strategy is to acknowledge the need to rest and set a specific time to snap the rut.

Most professional time management courses teach this lesson in some form or another.  In essence, we should force ourselves to indulge in our laziness, but only for a set period of time. It's OK to get stuck so long as you use that time to recharge.  In order to recharge you must disconnect and step away for a time. For example, if you find yourself at the end of the day, and see it was wasted on meaningless activities which are not moving your dreams forward, then it's time to schedule even more lazy time. Do not let yourself do anything productive.  Soon your mind will be screaming to make advancements.  If you do a little bit of work mixed with your leisure, you will exhaust your willpower quicker because you will trick your mind into thinking you can be productive and relax at the same time.  You cannot. Your work will suffer and your leisure will not relax you.

If you force yourself to be unproductive, this will create distaste for the lazy unproductive activity. More often than not you will realize the wasted opportunity and get unstuck. There will always be a need to disconnect from work, just make sure you do it completely.

2.    Stop planning.  Analysis by paralysis is a pervasive problem in many people. It is the misconception that planning and strategy are inherently productive activities. While critically vital, the planning stage must give way to action at frequently increasing intervals.  Otherwise, data-overload soon controls your mind, and you will be constantly plagued by second-guessing rather than jumping into a project and getting started. You will forget the major steps you need to take.  Data-overload is the enemy of brevity, swiftness and worst of all, immediate action.  Allow time for planning followed by immediate action.  Remember, you will never have a perfect amount of information, but luckily neither will your opponents and competitors.

3.    Prepare to act.  Preparation and analysis are not the same.  Analysis is often just another term for data-mining.  When you begin to gather too much information, eventually you will start collecting data which makes you doubt your position. Preparation however is the process of organizing for action. Implementing ideas into a first rough draft is preparation for meaningful writing. Sorting and executing vital first steps is meaningful long term activities. Analysis leads to wandering while preparation leads to focusing.

When you are stuck, stop planning and start preparing. Begin outlining your goals for an upcoming negotiation.  Execute the first step of your marketing plan. Etc.  Preparation beats talent when talent doesn't prepare.

Sometimes I find it difficult to transition from the analysis phase to the writing phase. When I am stuck in this rut, I just tell myself to "Write for the Trash".  This allows me to write anything no matter how incoherent just to get started.  So now I include a trash-draft stage.  A pre-first draft stage which gets me writing things down in a wild brainstorming fashion.  This activity frees my creative mind and I find the transition seamless.

**Action Step** - If you are stuck, remember it is temporary. You cannot be consistently creative but you also cannot be consistently stuck either.  Make sure you are preparing when you are stuck and sooner rather than later the creativity will flow. Use a trash draft, first draft, and final draft, three-step process to get out of the planning and analysis phase.


## J.A.M. Journal Writing Cue

**Write down three techniques to call upon when you are stuck. What activities get you recharged the quickest? List the three most enjoyable activities in which to indulge to unplug and get unstuck.**

**1.**


**2.**


**3.**


## Day 18 - How to benefit from Commitment Bias

In his book, The Influence of Persuasion, Dr. Cialdini describes the power of commitment as follows:

People are naturally indecisive. When deciding whether or not to buy a product or service, people will be very skittish. They will self-evaluate product or service and often they will seek to escape the situation with an excuse such as "let me think about it" or I have to speak too my wife etc. Every salesperson knows this is typically the kiss of death. High pressure salesmen may respond:

"No problem take all the time you want, but it may not be here tomorrow."

This is a transparent, aggressive tactic, which often defeats the intended result and reinforces the costumer's conviction to walk away. The product is now less important than the salesman's dishonesty. *People detest being sold but they love to buy.*

Dr. Cialdini suggests the more subtle approach of using commitment to close the deal.

Commitment bias is a much more subtle (sneaky) approach to closing a deal. Using this theory the salesman elicits a small commitment from the customer:

A recently rebuked salesman might say

"No problem, however, if you want to put a small refundable, deposit down on this I can hold it open for you for 24 hours".

Sometimes referred to as the "puppy dog effect" because of the effectiveness pet shops have with allowing the customer to take the cute puppy dog home for a couple of days.

Our bias towards commitment makes us very susceptible to this form of persuasiveness.

Studies show that the conversion rate (prospect to sale) when there is a small commitment is exponentially higher. It is much easier to sell a $1,000.00 upgrade when you have $100.00 then it is to "cold sell" a $1,000 product or service.

It is important to be aware of human psychology if you intend to interact and sell things to others. This book is focused on jump starting productivity, but part of your agenda should be dedicated to improving your understanding of why people buy or walk if you are in any type of business. The above referenced book is a great starting point.

### Action Step

Recognize the commitment bias and use that knowledge to stay out of bad deals. Utilize the commitment bias to convince clients/customers that your product/service is the best for them.

### J.A.M. Journal Writing Cue:

**The commitment bias is subtle but used in many types of sales. Identify transactions which convince you to take something for free or low cost in order to up sell you on a larger intended product.**

1.


2.


3.


## Day 19 Helping others achieve more.

*"Beginning today, treat everyone you meet as if they were going to be dead by midnight. Extend to them all the care kindness, and understanding you can muster, and do it all with no thought of any reward. Your life will never be the same again."* - Og Mandino.

The ultimate goal of this book is to get others motivated to pursue their professional dreams and desires. One of the questions I often find myself asking my clients associates and partners is a variation of

"What is our end goal here?"

Very often clients will come to see me with a multitude of entwined issues. After forty-five minutes of discussion about possible legal actions, remedies and solutions, clients are sometimes inundated by complex legalese, rules and information overload. If a client doesn't understand what the lawyer is telling them, it is ultimately the lawyer's fault. However, clients often combine various legal, factual and emotional statements together requiring complex discussion.

Utilizing a pre-determined set of preliminary questions, also known as the Socratic method of questioning, I typically help others focus on their goals and what they want to achieve. In order to simplify this interaction I start at the end and working backwards. I ask the client, "what is our end goal?" What is it we hope to achieve? Usually prospective client are surprised by bluntness of the question. But, by reframing the question I get the client to focus on the end-goal first. The client will usually say something akin to "I just want the bank to allow me to pay my mortgage (despite being in arrears)", or "I want to stop this person or corporation from interfering with my business." etc.

By allowing the client to identify their end-goal, they begin self-educating themselves. They start talking about facts and details directly related to this end goal rather than all the extraneous details that were derailing the conversation earlier. If they are talking about the bank and paying their mortgage, then many of the superfluous facts (my wife/husband needs to get a job) becomes less important. When the client verbalizes their goal, they are in effect narrowing the conversation for both of us.

This technique also works well with associates, other attorneys, and co-workers. I often get calls from attorneys asking for advice on how to handle a case, or seeking my advice about a legal issue. Many times, even the attorney who is trained at spotting relevant issues begins by including superfluous facts and issues. When I see this happening I typically ask the colleague to tell me what the client's end goal is.

### Action Step -

As Dr. Stephen Covey says in the 7 Habits, "begin with the end in mind". Whether you, a co-worker, teammate or friend are struggling with a difficult problem or project, step back and ask "what is our goal here?" Once the goal is verbalized and refined, start working backwards from the goal until you arrive at the first, simplest, next step and begin from there.

### J.A.M. Journal Writing Cue

**Before you begin working on today's projects, write down the ultimate end result you hope to achieve at project**

completion. **Create incremental steps working back from the end result and execute today.**

**End Result of Project is**

_____

1.


2.


3.


4.


5.

# THE FINAL TEN DAYS

*"There is no use, one cannot believe impossible things" said Alice.*

*I dare say you haven't had much practice, I did it for half an hour each day, sometimes I believed as many as six impossible things before breakfast." Answered the Queen of Hearts.* - Lewis Carroll Alice in Wonderland.

## Day 20 - Understanding the different types of confidence

As we final ten days in the JAM your productivity and organization skills have begun to improve exponentially and you will also notice that you are more confident in your professional and personal interactions as a result. Confidence and productivity go hand in hand. Whether the venue is professional confidence for massive business success, conversational confidence for success in public and intimate conversations, or social confidence for group interactions, confidence is the common denominator. Today, let's concentrate on the various types of confidence and see how we can further improve them.

**Professional Confidence** - There is no substitute for being a productive person in your work place. When people say "does what you love", they are not telling you to go and work from the beach in Maui. Doing what you love is actually a self-fulfilling form of confidence. It means understand the job you currently have completely. Now do whatever it takes to do that job to the best of your potential. Doing what you love means being productive and exceeding your potential in the job you currently do. Productive people, convert their time into money without thinking about it. They get lost in a state of high productivity called "flow state". Being in a flow state translates to doing more of what you love, being productive in the field of your choice.

Become an expert in your existing job. Be the first to arrive and the last to leave. Constantly read about your changing industry. If you absolutely despise your job you will quickly realize it when you become an expert at it. If you are now an expert at your job and still hate it, you will inevitably leave, so the decision becomes very easy. If you just grind it out Monday through Friday because you

51

need a paycheck, you will never experience your job as an expert. Therefore you will never have the confidence you need in business to do what you love. By becoming an expert in your job as quick as possible you will have the added benefit of knowing if you are in the right career. The best way to find a job you love is to become great at your job.

**Conversational Confidence** - The ability to talk freely and be relaxed in any discussion is an indispensable skill. Use these tips to increase conversational confidence:

1.      Practice conversations wherever you go.

2.      Learn to listen twice as much as you speak and respond with a summary of what you just heard.

3.      Look at people in the eye when meeting them, frequent eye contact (not maniacal staring) creates confidence.

4. Always repeat people's names while conversing at least three times during initial conversations.

5.      Summarize what you hear in your own words and ask open ended questions to learn more about people.

6.      Ask questions about the other person's thoughts and theories.

7.      If you feel a personal connection, always secure a way to follow-up and continue the discussion in the future.

8.      Do not to get uncomfortable by long pauses, lulls or silence in conversations.

I am often stricken green with envy by those people I see at parties who have nearly an endless array of topics to discuss. However, upon closer examination, conversational confidence is mostly the ability to assuage, acknowledge and listen to the other person.

A very effective technique to building conversational confidence is repeating the other persons point in a slightly different way, and then slowly and subtlety pushing your own agenda forward.

Conversational confidence is the ability to listen and be comfortable, and not always be thinking of the next thing to say. Open ended questions are questions that require more than just a yes or no answer. I.e. Tell me how you first got started in the Real Estate Business. Etc. Rather than thinking of an interesting or witty response, simply, restate what you have heard and offer your opinion i.e.

So you got started in the Real Estate business after your divorce, was it difficult to build a network when you started? Etc.

People often say "I just needed to vent". This is a sign that this person wants to have a conversation and doesn't want a dispute. You don't have to agree with everybody, but you should understand the points being made and repeat them back to the speaker.

Sometimes you just need to let people state their opinion. Not everything has to be a political debate. While we are on the subject it is always a good idea to avoid debates on Political views and religion whenever possible.

**Social Confidence** - The final piece of the confidence triad is social confidence. Closely related to conversational confidence, being comfortable in group settings require being comfortable with you as an individual. Let's say you are in a social gathering in which you know few or none of the people. Furthermore, you have some psychological baggage and feel you don't fit in. If you are overweight, tired or not dressed appropriately don't run from the fact. Emphasize it. A person who is confident (not arrogant) is fun. Self-depreciating humor used sparingly, breaks down walls and will help you avoid seeming arrogant.

Own who you are because there is nothing you can do at this moment to change. Be bold. Owning who you are, will make people gravitate towards you. I have seen truly interesting and fascinating people unable to work a room, and I have seen unassuming, timid people generate massive enthusiasm by barely speaking. The latter walks into a room head high chest out and proud of whom they are. They make eye contact and smile slightly. They are optimistic and happy to be in the moment. Social confidence has taught them to lock eyes nod at the right times, smile when appropriate and inevitable reach in for a hug or arm over the shoulder. Bold and proud of whom they are, the herd gathers round them and the interactions are effortless. Social confidence is not so much about words as it is about actions, posture and attitude.

**Action Step**- Practice the three confidences today and for the rest of the week. Come in early and stay late. Converse as much as possible. Listen and ask open ended questions. Finally, seek out social gatherings. Be bold and proud of who you are.

### J.A.M. Journal Writing Cue:

**Create a schedule to forces you into social interactions aimed at improving your confidence. Toastmasters, rotary organizations and other networking groups are excellent examples. List three social groups to join this month:**

**1.**

**2.**

**3.**

**How will you improve your confidences during these interactions?**

### Day 21 - Believe you can win, proclaim victory, and work towards victory.

*"You are naturally great and your potential for greatness is ever ready."*- Christian Larson.

Yesterday we focused on improving confidence in three areas of our lives. Today we need to extend that confidence to our system of goal achievement. Having a goal is a great basic level step to becoming focused. However, having a system of goal achievement, such as the JAM is exceptional. A system requires confidence and belief that you will succeed so long as you follow the pattern of progress. You must believe that you can win in every transaction or competition that you undertake. Always be learning and always believe you can win in any interaction.

Donald Trump is a great example of a blindly confident and savage personality type. Trump proclaims he will win early and often. He posts to twitter daily showing how far ahead he is in his presidential bid. He creates a perception that there is no point in voting for anyone other than him. And his belief becomes a reality through his confidence and persistence.

The late, great Mohamed Ali proclaimed he was the world's greatest boxer even before he was. This supreme confidence coupled with a public pronouncement is a factor in the most successful people from Arnold Schwarzenegger to Floyd Mayweather. Sharing your dream of success with the public is a very effective, self-accountability tool that we should use often.

Confidence without substance is arrogance. All of the above mentioned titans in their field, worked tirelessly to back up their trade. Trump, Ali, Mayweather are also known to back up their confidence with unrivaled hard work. They are well-known to be tireless, never-sleeping, super-humans by those who know them. Bruce Lee and Arnold Schwarzenegger accomplished phenomenal feats because they focused every day, every hour and every minute on progress. But it was their combination of confidence and self-proclamation to the world that made them titans in their respective industries.

**Action Steps**- Study the industry leaders in your field. Always be a student throughout your life and study the legends every chance you get. Were they timid and unassuming? Or rather, were they bold and confident? Did they out-work the competitors at every turn and were they never satisfied?

Select leaders from the best in the world and implement their lessons during the next thirty days. Be supremely confident and experience the glory of unrivaled success.

### J.A.M. Journal Writing Cue

**Select a legend in the following fields: Business, Politics, Sports and your industry. List the names and some of the supreme qualities that they possessed throughout their lives.**

**Business-**


**Politics-**


**Sports-**


**My Industry** _____


### Day 22 - Learn Once, Do Once, Teach Once.

Yesterday, we spoke about the necessity of being a lifelong student of the world. "Always Be Learning" is a much more powerful and rewarding mantra than "Always Be Closing" from the famous speech by Alec Baldwin, the cut throat salesman, in the movie <u>Glengarry, Glen Ross</u>. Learn every day, implement what you have learned, and teach it to others, only then will you truly own a skill. This simple rule used in business, education and the military, is extremely effective when tackling new challenges.

At a recent seminar I explained this rule to the audience as follows:

1. Learn once - Put in the time to learn a skill or task. Read, research and review the skill. Deconstruct the skill into its smallest

elements. Create three aspects of the skill and begin working towards each of the three aspects. .

New attorneys often come to me and ask me how to begin work on complicated cases. Despite having extensive training in law school, when it comes to real world planning, key legal tools are left out by the professors.

So I begin at the basic level, spotting the most important issues in a case. Next we move on to the 3 most important statutes, case law or common law (general) principles. This act of narrowing the focus to only three elements is greatly effective in streamlining the process.

The skill here is "writing effective legal memos" We identify three major principals or points that need to be communicated in the memo, and finally we frame the legal issues.

2.      Do Once - Practice, practice, practice. After learning the basics we need to "do once". The word once implies doing the task correctly. Not perfectly, but correctly. Sticking with the legal memo from above this "do once" step can look like this:

Doing once is an action step. J.A.M. is designed to get to action steps as soon as possible. Often associates will get lost in drafting the memo perfectly, selecting the latest and best case law and becoming overly comfortable in the drafting process. Many young associates skip the presentation step in favor of more practice and they soon develop analysis paralysis. When you fail to rehearse in front of an audience you fail to commit to anything. Your mind is content that you have unlimited time to present unlimited issues and arguments. Without doing once the project is untested.

The Associate has learned how to write the memo, and he has practiced. The associate will now present the memo to me or audience and he/she will be open to constructive criticism.

Let's use a different example, How to get started as a writer. Step one Write something. When I decided to write this book I had dozens of pages of notes, index cards, binders, voice recordings and videos. My mind was content, and comfortable in the process of gathering and sorting information. While research is vital, I had tricked my mind into believing that research was an action step and not merely a planning step. When it came down to writing, the doing of the task, my mind fought back. I would allow myself to accept any excuse not to write.

My mind wanted to read more, and do more research, review and refine my notes and otherwise delay the doing of the task. Something wonderful happened when I finally started writing however, actually doing the task became easier and easier. The resistance became weaker than none existence. Eventually I would reach the ultimate state, the Flow State.

What was once a fear, "am I forgetting something" now became an advantage "I am committing to something". However, without this "doing step" and allowing others to review and hold me accountable then the project could never be completed. Overcoming this barrier was difficult, but became easier as I implemented the self-same rules which I am now writing about. Once I finished writing this book, it became a tool from which I could now "teach once".

3.      Teach Once. As a former teacher, current attorney and future author (hopefully) I have availed myself of countless opportunities to teach others. I teach through the various seminars and presentations that I give throughout the year. I use interesting stories and anecdotes while I teach others about starting their own business. Nowadays there are countless avenues for teaching other your ideas and theories. Teaching can also be done through social posts, blogging and vlogging in addition to in-person interaction.

It's amazing how the teaching step codifies and improves an idea. I see my writing and presentations improve every time I teach from it. The improvement is sometimes as the result of input from the audience and sometimes from the result of my inner self-correcting voice. This is an invaluable step in the January Advantage Method. All of us have already accomplished great things that others can learn from. Seek out any opportunity you can to teach others how you achieved certain goals and met certain challenges in your life and your knowledge and confidence will increase exponentially.

**Action Step** - Today you will learn once, by learning or improving your knowledge of a certain skill. Deconstruct the skill into smaller steps and implement it. Begin projects as soon as practical. No one has perfect information at the time they decide to act and be aware that neither will you. Once you have a good understanding of the task, schedule time to implement it and do the task. Most importantly, seek feedback and constructive criticism. Everyone hates this step but it is imperative to the doing step.

### J.A.M. Journal Writing Cue

Select a task that you are already good at, or a recent accomplishment which took a lot of work. Try to think of ways you can explain your skill to others. Odds are, you have dozens if not hundreds of useful skills that could benefit others. Give it away for free and watch the rewards of teaching once come back a hundred fold.

### Day 23 - Create "Anchor Events" in your schedules to make your week more meaningful and productive.

Gain control of your schedule and eliminate distractions. I often envy my law partner when it comes to scheduling. She is able to keep her schedule neat and clean with lots of open spaces. I, on the other hand, have a myriad of tasks and reminders as well as recurring events that pop-up whenever I open the calendar. Different colors attributed to events to denote priority make for an assault on the eyes when opened. But my schedule works for me and her schedule meets her needs.

The one thing we both have is fixed events. Anchor events, or fixed events, are recurring tasks that appear in our calendar.

Anchor events should also be used for items such as gym and fitness, weekly review and other productivity tasks. Recall the incremental checklist we compiled at the beginning of the J.A.M. Some of those elements should start becoming routine. These can now be converted into anchor items in your schedule. Here is an example of my schedule with anchor events:

1.    Monday morning from 8-10 is a no email zone for me. I will work on the week's most difficult project and let the calls go to voicemail. This is part of my overall plan to work at 110% on Monday so that I have control of the week by at least Wednesday.

2.    Tuesday from 10-11 a.m. I update my billable sheets and invoices to clients and review old email. I also use Tuesday morning for office meetings to get everyone on track.

3.    Wednesday from 11-12. I have similar fixed events such as marketing and networking throughout the week as well. These events are already present in my schedule and I do everything I can to schedule new tasks no matter how important around these fixed events. These events are improvement events (gym and fitness). These events are so important that I make alternative times if I miss them.

4.    Monday 5 pm is a set time for 30 minutes of strength training? I also set an alternative time of Wednesday at 7 p.m. should I miss the Monday session for any reason.

Setting self-improvements tasks as fixed items on the schedule with alternative dates is an effective tool to daily progression.

Tip- Look Forward Calendar Review - To get your calendar neater I suggest making a weekly anchor event to do a one week look forward review. For example, on Saturday I review my calendar and compare this Saturday to next Saturday. I make sure that all my fixed tasks are clear and have alternate dates. Then I move on to Sunday comparing it to next Sunday and finally,

Monday. The "one-week look-forward" is a great way to spot potential conflicts and it also plants upcoming activities in my subconscious.

If I have done my week-forward review and I have a court appearance on Thursday, I will remember this is my subconscious (usually). I may not remember the time, but I will know that Thursday is either partly or fully booked.

At the end of your week ask yourself, "What anchor tasks are simply not working in their allotted time slots?" "When can these be rescheduled?", "Are my tasks congruent with the events I enjoy whether they be professional or not? In the beginning there will be a lot of deleting and moving around, but soon the calendar will start to function as a welcome companion rather than a ruthless task master.

**Action Step** - As we begin to identify highly productive tasks it is now time to convert these bursts of energy into Anchor items on the weekly schedule. Maximize your strongest tasks and most productive hours of the day to get the most out of these surges in productivity. These items have been proven as effective and they require prolonged commitment. As you remove items from the incremental checklist add new items to test their effectiveness.

### J.A.M. Journal Writing Cue

**Make a list of five Anchor events (self- improvement items) and schedule them along with alternate dates in your weekly calendar.**

1.

2.

3.

4.

5.

## Day 24 Coming back after a break -

By this point in the J.A.M. you have experienced a significant gain in energy, productivity and motivation. The most frustrating thing is that motivation is a finite resource. It ebbs and flows over time. The reason we perform at optimal levels during the first month of the year is because we strive to be our "best self" during this time, we combine that desire with focused action. No wonder we soon exhaust ourselves and fall back to our old habits by February or sooner.

Coming back after a slump is vital to maintaining momentum. In order to anticipate our inevitable slump we must plan accordingly. We can even learn to embrace the upcoming loss of motivation as it is part of the natural cycle to replenish your energy.

In the beginning of the J.A.M. we set up an incremental, micro-action, checklist. Some of those items have now been converted into anchor items in our calendar.

When you realize you are in a slump, it is time to break out the list of small baby steps from the beginning of this experiment. Seek out the simplest incremental steps. Sometimes, simply reorganizing my work area can get me back on track. This will not only jumpstart your creativity sooner, it will also keep you moving forward. You will also remain confident because you know that you will always have a list of proven, relatively simple steps to keep the productivity moving forward.

**Action Step**- After a period of non-productive activity, such as binge watching our favorite show on Netflix, or a three day video game marathon, revert back to proven techniques. Today go back to your incremental, micro-action, checklist and try to complete simple ten minute tasks. These tasks have already been vetted and proven to keep you moving forward.

### J.A.M. Journal Writing Cue

**A question to ask after a slump/break - Are there any projects which have not moved forward in a week or more? Are these projects still worth doing? If so, what small incremental**

**task can I do today to move this project forward? Make a list of micro actions that get you motivated after a slump.**

1.

2.

3.

4.


### Day 25 Using down-time wisely

Ideally, the J.A.M. could keep us highly motivated for thirty consecutive days. Ideally, it could guarantee us at least one full month of increased productivity throughout the year. But by now you know that the J.A.M. is not so much a method bound by the days on a calendar as it is a concept to steadily move forward towards our goals, recognize our potential, and capture the momentum to take immediate action.

Inevitably, our motivation will wane and we will experience periods of low/no activity. It is important to create a plan for down-time in order to keep moving towards our goals. When you expect a downturn in productivity we can prepare a contingency plan to get us through this slump.

When I first tested the J.A.M. I experimented on myself. I hypothesized that my downturn in productivity would occur at or near the end of January. To my surprise, I found my motivation slacking as soon as the end of the second week (day 14). Instead of viewing this loss of motivation as the end of a cycle, I saw it more as a plateau or period of adjustment. Let's face it, if I wrote a book about the first two weeks of January I would have to change the title.

Since we are all different, we must perform an initial J.A.M. experiment to isolate when your specific plateau will occur. You must track your own progress to pinpoint when you slump is likely to occur.

Once I knew that this would be a plateau in my productivity I implemented a contingency strategy to get me through the next fifteen days. Knowing this, I can plan properly for every January. I don't fight this downturn in productivity rather I adjust my approach. During this mid- month of slower motivation, I steer away from the creative aspects and I concentrate on routine improvements.

By concentrating on maintaining the status quo and not losing ground, you are better prepared for making huge gains when your motivation kicks in. By creating a list of simple down time activities and techniques I always feel that I am making progress no matter how minimal. Some of the items on my list are:

- Re-read and summarize interesting articles and books;

- Organize material for easy retrieval later;

- Clear, clean and organize all of my work spaces;

- Combine like objects in their own space;

- Purge, purge, purge eliminate outdated information and objects. If you have not used or referenced an item in six months it is likely to be trash.

- Consolidate and organize digital files and media

In the Seven Habits of Highly effective people, Dr. Stephen Covey tells us that our down time is the time to "sharpen the saw, and work on our strengths". I make progress on the mundane and I increase the efficiency of how I perform daily activities. It is much less work to streamline an existing procedure then it is to create entirely new systems.

Another way to get out of a slump is to revisit and or reactivate some systems which have worked in the past. Some examples are:

- Follow up on leads to grow your network;

- Review account receivables;

- Make phone calls on overdue invoices;

- Restart gym routines;

- Improve/learn online marketing;

- Revise checklists and purge out dated lists.

Instead of focusing on large gains during the middle of January just try to maintain my progress.

My all-time favorite author Stephen King says that when he has writer's block, he stays productive by going back over his work and eliminating useless words. This is one of the most frequent tips he gives to aspiring writers. Coincidently if you are serious about becoming an author I highly recommend his book <u>On Writing by Stephen King.</u>

The mid-month plateau is a perfect time to go back and edit our work. It is a good time to organize head notes and refine footnotes. Compile research in to binders for easier access and purge outdated data and information. Improve transitions between paragraphs and chapters and edit, proof read and refine. I find this time to be a welcome break from the furious brainstorming of creative writing.

**Action Steps**: Train yourself to expect and anticipate plateaus. Look forward to a time when you can adjust and focus on organizing and correcting, rather than producing and creating. Use the down turn in productivity to maintain the status quo and not lose the gains made in the first half of the month. Prepare for the inevitable surge of productivity that is sure to follow. Always remember motivation is a finite and exhaustible resource. Create a plan to move forward while your resource replenishes yourself. Avoid the temptation of allowing yourself to relax in a state of un-productivity.

## J.A.M. Journal Writing Cue

**Create a list of ten down-time activities that you can implement the next time you encounter a slump in productivity:**

1.                          2.


3.                          4.


5.                          6.


7.                          8.


9.                          10.


## Day 26 Dealing with Doubt

There is one sure way to failure, allow self-doubt to derail you. Today as I drove through the park to go to my favorite café to work on my book, I was suddenly hit with a wave of doubt. Questions about my perceived lack of dedication and qualifications invaded my thoughts.

"Why am I spending my time on this project?"

no one will read my book;

I need to start over.

This project is taking away time for what is really important.

In a matter of seconds, self-doubt nearly convinced me to give up over a year of hard work, research and writing.

Self-doubt is an enemy of confidence and a roadblock to momentum. Self-doubt also has a benefit. It is a safety mechanism to make us rethink certain causes of action. However when it comes to our profession and advancing our dreams odds are that we have selected pious goals and the self-doubt is simply acting as a way to avoid the hard work and dedication needed to reach our goals. Self-doubt pretends to protect us from (imagined) embarrassment and criticism.

Doubt must be crushed, eviscerated and destroyed. We must recognize this enemy and immediately employ our mental defenses against it. It is not easy to crush doubt, but understanding it can be the first step in dealing with doubt.

Similar to procrastination, doubt destroys creativity. However, where procrastination convinces you there will be time, later in the future, to finish the project, doubt tries to convince you to toss the whole project in the garbage and give up the endeavor entirely. Because of that, doubt is much worse than procrastination. If procrastination wins, our projects, dreams and goals will be delayed, but if self-doubt wins are dreams may die.

We must develop tactics to control the battlefield when the enemy, self-doubt, appears.

**Tip 1. Defeat Doubt by Changing the scenery, go somewhere new, make an adventure out of it.**

One way to change the environment is to change the area where you normally work. If you typically write at your favorite coffee shop, switch to a new location. Change your surroundings and the people you are likely to interact with. Make a mini-adventure out of finding new places to be creative. The first step in overcoming doubt is to change the scenery.

### Tip 2 Defeat Doubt by conceding the fact and continuing despite it.

The second technique to trigger when doubt arises is to answer doubt with the best type of counter argument,

"even if true, so what?"

Frequently used in the legal profession, this question is highly effective in disabling an opponent. I will often concede my opponents point rather than directly refuting it. Once conceded, I immediately follow it with "even if true ....", my adversaries point has lost merit, and I have earned credibility at the same time. So as an author, I may be faced with doubt in the following form:

"Why am I writing this if No one will ever read it?"

When this occurs my response is simple

"Even if true, so what?"

At the very least this project will be completed and I can begin my next project and the next and the next. Eventually, at least one other person will read what I write, even if by accident. Doubt has no rebuttal for this reply.

Even if true… I will read it. Even if true… I must continue to write it because I want to read it. I want to hold a completed project in my hand. Maybe no one will read my first book but maybe two people will read my second book. I can't get to my second book unless I finish this one. These arguments are irrefutable and defeat doubt.

## Tip 3 Relax and wander

Doubt and discouragement go hand-in-hand. Don't let self-doubt destroy what you have already accomplished. Sometimes distractions are needed.

If self-doubt is particularly strong, allow yourself to be distracted. Start a new project if absolutely necessary, but whatever you do, do not abandon what you have worked on. Relax and allow yourself to be temporarily distracted. If you had a writing session scheduled and you were looking forward to a huge amount of progress on a particular day, do your best to overcome doubt. However, if you cannot be productive, allow yourself time to be temporarily distracted, but return to your work even if just for a moment until your inspiration inevitably returns.

If you reach a plateau or block to your creativity, the best advice is to simply "own it". Relax and allow yourself to be temporarily stalled. If it is writers block, don't stop writing completely just stop working on your main project and write about whatever you want. Perhaps there is a completely unrelated story or there is an anecdote that you want to write about and develop, then work on that new project for a time.

The legendary author Toni Morrison stated that she wrote her first book primarily because, "I wanted to read it." Create for yourself first and foremost. Perhaps others will read your work in the future and perhaps not. This is how I deal with doubt after I have committed to a project and if you are holding something in your hands at this point it seems to have worked out well.

## J.A.M. Journal Writing Cue

**Identify three self-doubt questions which could arise during the course of your next project. By writing them down**

**they will lose power over you in the future. That which you anticipate can be avoided and defeated.**

1.


2.


3.


## Day 27 - Never Seek Pity, Always seek an Advantage

Average People seek Pity. Great people seek an edge or advantage often. I think about an edge or advantage often. I constantly ask myself "what edge or advantage do I have?" in any particular negotiation, or transaction.

Average people desire sympathy, compassion and pity. These people often substitute complaints instead of action, excuses instead of taking responsibility, and emotion instead of logical reasoning. The pity group is one we all belong to at different times throughout our lives.

There are times when we all need to "vent", gossip and complain. Afterward we need to recognize this for what it is, a non-productive trap, as we recharge our self-motivation mechanism. The pity group is often depressed and pessimistic. There are those people who constantly post negative emotions on Facebook and social media. They love telling you how they feel, and how they have been cheated. They level complaints against the weather, their boss and their romantic partners. The pity group expects you to "be there for them". They feed off emotion and seek validation. The pity group gets emotionally "hurt" when you don't have time to listen to them. They need you to tell them that everything will be all right.

Do we need to support our friends in times of need? of course. But we need to empower them and move on with our own goals and dreams as soon as possible. They must decide to continue on the journey with us or stay where they are. Do not feed the pity group. They will drain you and drag you down with them.

Great people always seek an advantage. While the pity group bemoans their faith, the great people see an opportunity to learn, grow and adjust. We must be in this mindset as much as possible. When we feel discouraged ask

"how can I avoid this in the future?"

"What plans or preparations can I make to anticipate the current setback and avoid it?"

Every difficult task is an opportunity. Every pitfall a lesson to be learned and taught to others. Wealthy people know how to make money in good and bad markets equally well because the words good and bad are meaningless. They seek an edge, recognize a pattern and execute a proven plan. The wealthy seek an advantage in all market conditions. If a plan is not working as intended they adjust and compensate accordingly. When they succeed, great people immediately replay the scenario that led to this victory over and over in their head. They make detailed notes and plan to implement the strategies in the future. They are alert for a similar opportunity in which they can repeat this success.

Few, if any, people can perpetually maintain an ever-vigilant mentality but we must strive to spend all of our productive, energetic time thinking about advantages. Waking up early is an advantage if we use the extra hours productively. Staying up late is an advantage if we maximize our productivity and out-perform the competitors. Asking for a discount in any and all interactions is an advantage of bargaining. The J.A.M. is a thirty- day period where you must seek a daily advantage in all that you say, learn and do.

Try to surround yourself with high-achievers and you will see what I mean when I say that successful people are always looking for an edge or an advantage. Seek a daily advantage but also seek friends and colleagues who enjoy competition as well. Seek acquaintances that are much more successful than you and learn as much as you can from them. Watch what advantages they have over others and emulate them. Observe and learn from the way in which they solve problems and negotiate daily transactions. Mentors have been the foundation of accelerated learning since we began to live in communities and for good reason.

**Action Step** - Identify your pity seeking friends and eliminate them from your daily life. Identify those people who are successful and always seeking opportunity. Emulate and learn from the latter group and limit the exposure to the former. Seek to become a person who seeks an edge or advantage in all things and endeavors.

**J.A.M. Journal Writing Cue**

**Create a list of five people who you hope to include within your circle of influence as mentors this year. You may have personal access to them or you may only be able to research them, nevertheless choose five people this year with qualities you admire. Watch and learn how they seek and edge or advantage and write down the strongest characteristics or qualities that they utilize in daily activities:**

**1.** _____ Defining Characteristic or quality that I can emulate

_____

**2.** _____ Defining Characteristic or quality that I can emulate

_____

**3.** _____ Defining Characteristic or quality that I can emulate

_____

**4.** _____ Defining Characteristic or quality that I can emulate

_____

**5.** _____ Defining Characteristic or quality that I can emulate

_____

**Day 28 - Values are the guides of our life. Reviewing our values provides daily reminders of what is important in our lives.**

*"Do not be too moral you might cheat yourself out of much life. Aim high above morality, create your own code. Be not simply good; be good for something".* - Thoreau

Now that you have selected a group of people as your mentors to emulate, what values do you admire in the people you have selected?

Can you see those values as being your values no or in the near future?

Self-evaluation is a critical tool to success. However, like everything else, we must not overly indulge in introspection lest we become a wandering philosopher of 1,000 theories and 0 experiments. Once a year I like to disconnect and reflect on my life for several days. I re-read my journals and think about where I am in life. During this process I am looking at the things that I value most in life. As I wrote this sentence I am sitting on a beach in Malibu reconnecting with my values.

My values typically remain the same from year to year, Reading, healthy living, leading an organized life, being a knowledgeable attorney, enjoying travel and times with friends and family. After this retreat, I come back invigorated and determined to accomplish my vision and mission in life.

Sometimes, my values will change depending on life events and my maturity. Our maturity and responsibilities greatly shape our value system and priorities in life. For example, before I was married my values were different then after I had a family. It should be done at the end of the J.A.M. but it is always good to be cognizant of what drives us in life.

Once you isolate a set of values that will guide you in the upcoming year, create an acronym to follow and keep you on track. One particular year I wrote the following acronym to remind me of my life's values:

R.E.D.O.

Read often and voraciously,

Exercise and train often so the body can be stronger and faster than it was last year,

Diet and nutrition are the most important factors in a healthy and energetic lifestyle. Be cognizant of good nutrition when food shopping, eating out and socializing.

Organization is the first step to preparation and preparation beats talent nine times out of ten when talent doesn't prepare.

I used this index card as a daily reminder of the values that I consider important and follow it as often as I can. On the back of the card I place an "x" every time I remember to reference the card and enact an action in accordance with one of my values.

**Action Step -** Allocate time throughout the year to indulge in deep introspection. Identify the values in your life that are important to you. Write these values on an index card and refer to it throughout the year. Every time you act in accordance with your values, place an x on the back of the card. Live in accordance with your values and you success and productivity will soar in these areas.

## J.A.M. Journal Writing Cue

**Plan out a week for yourself this year where you can get away from it all. Do not include this as your vacation time or family time as there are other priorities, schedules and goals involved in those activities. Rather plan a retreat to be alone with your thoughts and focus on your life values.**

**Date of this year's introspection retreat**

_____

**Place**

_____

**Length of trip**

_____

**What improvements will I focus on during this yearly adventure?**

---

### Day 29 - Desensitization- eliminate shyness, anxiety and uncertainty in 30 seconds flat.

*"Nothing Splendid has ever been achieved except by those who dared believe that something inside them was superior to circumstance."* - Bruce Barton.

If I could go back in time twenty years, and say three words to my younger-self, I would shout DESENSITIZATION three times. My younger self would probably flee in panic at that point, however the intention was good. This is the most important single element of my success. Desensitization, the elimination of over-sensitivity, is a common, indispensable, element of the most successful people in the world.

Simply, not giving a damn is one of the best mindsets to be in when dealing with an overwhelming majority of situations. This is very difficult to do when you are an inexperienced entrepreneur but as soon as you can break out from this state of tameness success is assured. The sooner you can quiet down that inner coward, your progress will be exponential.

I will never forget how my success in Court increased once I stopped worrying about what the others in the courtroom were thinking. My focus and confidence soared once I understood, that my adversary, the judge and the jurors are regular people like me, who make mistakes and ask questions. My preparation became so much sharper when I decided that I was not going to jump at every request made by my client. I learned to engage the Judge in polite but firm conversations rather than fearful responses. Most importantly, when indecisive, I simply chose to act with confidence despite a lack of knowledge or concern for what others thought of me, and that has made all the difference.

When we are in our twenties and early thirties the most important area to implement desensitization is in our social context. We are entirely obsessed with how our friends and family will judge our actions. We find comfort in flirtations, but must seek discomfort in engagement. Fortunately, our good looks and youth allow us to indulge this non-productive exercise and still manage to attract the opposite sex. However, imagine the untold success if you could tap into desensitization at this early stage. Imagine the abundance you could experience if you could quiet your inner critic and live a life of confidence as early as twenty-one years of age.

When we reach our thirties we are typically entering into our careers and it is at this time that desensitization would yield its largest benefit in our professional lives. Lacking experience is often seen as a weakness, but by utilizing desensitization to quiet our inner coward, our lack of experience becomes a strength because we are expected to make mistakes. Don't be afraid to ask many stupid questions about work. Don't be embarrassed when you realize you don't fit in a certain company. Desensitize yourself when you ask for a raise, or promotion. Be brave, be bold and be decisive. Rarely if ever, will a mistake at this level have catastrophic effects, but the upside will be tremendous. You will frequently be forgiven because of your lack of experience and your accomplishments will skyrocket.

I need to increase desensitization in my life. You will notice that the older some people are, the less they care about what others think. The reason for this is that they have discovered the secret of desensitization. The truth is, that the power of desensitization will manifest itself if we live long enough, however, embrace desensitization today and begin experiencing its liberating power in your lives.

**Action Step** - Desensitize now. Wherever you are, make a vow for the rest of the week/month that you will stop caring what other people think. Act on your instincts. Quiet down your inner coward and be bold. Life is unpredictable. You will age and grow weak. Those people who were able to silence you with gossip and nasty looks could care less about your future. You will learn that people care about what you do much less than you think.

Desensitize yourself to the thoughts of others. Be a trailblazer, and you will, in-turn conquer your haters with actions instead of words.

## J.A.M. Journal Writing Cue

**Select three areas in your life where you can benefit from desensitization. List these areas and how map out a plan of how you will empower yourself to progress these areas without worrying about the criticism of others.**

1. _____ **Desensitize by**

2. _____ **Desensitize by**

3. _____ **Desensitize by**

## Day 30 - Mapping your ideal days to create realistic daily plans.

As you the end the 1st JAM session, you have begun to develop techniques that can assure consistent productivity in your career, health and happiness. You now realize that potential is far greater. Today's exercise is to combine what we have learned into a repeatable plan for daily productivity.

As we refine and perfect the techniques that we have learned so far ask yourself:

"what would your perfect day look like in terms of maximizing productivity?"

The JAM is all about isolating our best selves at our most hopeful and motivated, then spotting a pattern to trigger that advantage whenever we want. If we can isolate what makes January work, it is possible to repeat it throughout the year. One tool to use in isolating our most productive pattern is mapping our day.

Mapping the day is different than constructing to-do lists or writing down monthly, weekly and yearly goals . Mapping has two components. An imagined "perfect day" and then a realistic day.

For the first step of this exercise create an hour by hour list of the perfect day. Assume unlimited energy, no distraction and no other obligations. Assume a perpetual, positive, can-do attitude for the entire day. In other words we are writing down a nearly un-attainable schedule. The idea here is to visualize what a day would look like in a perfect version. I once sat planed a perfect day in which I had limitless motivation and energy. It looked like this:

## <u>ANATOMY OF THE PERFECT SATURDAY</u>

A.M. 8-9 Out of bed and start being creative. Write 5-10 pages of new content.

9-10 Light breakfast and update all schedules for the upcoming month.

10-12  Gym, Cardio and strength training.

12-1 p.m.      Hot shower, eat a healthy kale salad with some skirt steak for lunch.

1-3     Networking with potential clients and connectors.

3-4     Marketing and updating social media.

4-5     Read 1 book a day.

5-7     Dinner with family, recreation.

7-9     Final writing/creative sessions. Draft another ten pages of error free content.

9-10    Evening Networking over drinks.

The above plan is unattainable, at least for me it is.    It requires limitless energy, but more importantly it requires perfect timing and scheduling.  Any activity that requires the input of others is very difficult to schedule and therefore it requires flexibility which this schedule lacks.

So why partake in the exercise? By mapping out what a perfect day looks like, we can select the most important events and fit them into a realistic, but still highly productive, schedule.

## Selecting high value items and creating fallback events to maintain momentum.

The above map teaches me some of the values I wish to focus on, being creative, networking and reading on the weekend. I also want to try and fit in some exercise if possible.  My map tells me my high value items are writing (2 entries) Reading (2 entries) Networking (3 entries including dinner with family/friends). My map tells me that my important value is exercise (1 entry early in the AM). Having identified these aspects of a perfect day, we now owe it to ourselves to create a schedule for Saturday that has at least some of these items as "Anchor" events.

Planning for the JAM will inevitably lead to many amazingly productive days, but we cannot achieve perfect productivity overnight. Using the above map would quickly lead to failure.  So I will try to select three items from the list of four as anchor items.  To insure the greatest chances of success, I will also choose an alternative, minimum, fallback position for each anchor item.  For example if I chose to commit to one hour of reading on Saturday, I will also add a fallback position to listen to thirty minutes of an audio book if I can't accomplish the primary task.  By selecting this fallback I can still keep the momentum going forward and in a straight line.

Based on the values in the above map, I can select three anchor items, and minimum fallback positions i.e.:

1. Read 40 pages /Audio Books 30 min.  2. One Hour writing/30 minutes of editing or research and 3. 1 Hour training at the gym /30 minutes of some type of physical activities.

A recent Saturday which I considered productive, developed as follows:

5:00 A.M. - Out of bed with high energy. listened to some Motivational/inspirational podcasts as I got ready for the day.

8-9 - Head out to my favorite coffee shop, was able to write for over one hour. Developed several new concepts and topics. (It is not even 10 a.m. and I have already hit two of my three high value items today reading/pod casts and writing).

9-10 - Typically, I avoid the office on the weekends, but I did spend an unanticipated hour at the office today meeting a new client who had an emergency.

10-12- Inevitable slowdown of the day to finish tasks and chores like food shopping, laundry cleaning etc.

As the day progressed, I had some creative ideas which I jotted down and put in my writing binder for later research. I can't emphasize how good it feels to have a system ready to catch random thoughts and ideas throughout the day and then to actually use it.

Snack - Ate some yogurt raisins throughout the day which kept my energy up.

11-12 P.M.  Homemade Lunch.  I was able to resist the strong urge to eat out for lunch.  Being able to eat well at home is also a mood booster in addition to helping me stay healthy.

12-1 Reflective meditation and quiet time.

1-3 Dedicated some time to my hobby which is building computers. Picked up some parts at the store took my time and lingered in the aisles studying motherboards and CPU performance charts.  Even though this is moving my hobby forward I really can't justify this trip to the store as anything else than self-indulgence.

2-3 A great gym workout. A combination of cardio, free weights, three machines to work the chest and arms.

4-6 Nonproductive time (need to shorten this is the future).

6-7 My second writing session of the day was also productive. A rarity for me. Usually, my second Saturday session is for editing organizing and reading, so this was a bonus. Good thing my lap top still had some battery life left.

Journaling and reflection. Preparing for Sunday.

Bonus- I resisted the high calorie Chi tea Late because of the gym guilt and went with a black coffee with nutmeg. I probably won't sleep well but I stayed true to my goal to stay healthy.

**Action Step**. Map a perfect, proactive day for each day of the week. As you achieve high energy and high productivity days, map these retroactively in your journal. Compare the two maps to create a challenging yet Realistic strategy wherein you can meet and exceed all of your high value items.

## J.A.M. Journal Writing Cue

Map your perfect day listing your anchor items and fall back positions to assure continued productivity.

## The Final days and beyond: The Battle plan for repeatable productivity

*"Fear less, hope more. Eat less, chew more. Whine less, breathe more. Talk less, say more. Love more and all good things will be yours."* - Swedish proverb.

As we reflect on what we have accomplished in the last month, we can begin to see our values emerge into a system of goal achievement and not just a list of random wishes or impossible goals. We have customized a plan to tap into our most productive self. The problem, and the impetus for writing this book, was to develop a repeatable plan to execute after the first 30 days of the month. In order to effectively achieve this goal we must treat this time as a battle. The enemy is our relentless desire to go back to the status quo. However, we are fighting for a future in which all of our goals and dreams can be fulfilled. To win this battle, we must take what we learned and extend the JAM in to the next thirty days. If we abide by the mantra of Learn Once, Do Once, Teach Once, then the first thirty days of the J.A.M. was the learning once and the next thirty will be the execution of the good habits we have developed.

The thirty tips in the JAM are interchangeable tools. Some days you may use only one of them. Hopefully most days you will implement several a day, every day. The rules are also interchangeable. This is especially true once you learned the basics. For example, a morning routine is created and improved throughout the year. The J.A.M. journal is a critical starting point, but once created, it becomes automatic and no longer an item to be focused on.

In summary, we now have the plans and ideas to continue being motivated and successful and highly productive for thirty days at a time all year long. Throughout the month we have recognized the amazing power of three and we have utilized savagery as opposed to tameness, desensitization as opposed to apology and seeking an advantage as opposed to seeking comfort. When I entered my second thirty days of the JAM I was able to interchange the tools I had learned to fit my current challenges. The following is my approach in the second JAM session:

The most useful elements to enact in the second thirty days are:

1. Activate and stick to the morning routine (Day 30);

2. Create and improve Anchor items in your daily schedule (Day 23);

3. Desensitize yourself, always. (Day 29);

4. Always seek an advantage and opportunity to learn, be curious (Intro);

5. Never leave a project unimproved (Day 1);

6. Use Timers to stay on Task (Day 6);

7. Continue with your daily savings plan (Day 7);

8. Develop good habits and smash bad habits (Day 11);

9. Recognize and improve upon your strengths (Day 12);

10. Build and improve the three confidences, Conversation, Professional and Social (Day 20).

In the second thirty days you must be relentless in your attacks and demand more from yourself. Now that you have embraced a savage mentality, you can construct relentless attacks in business and in your social situations. When you set your mind on a goal, you need to develop a plan of attack. You must train yourself to think that the relentless pursuit of success requires action every day. A relentless mentality means that there is never a failure, simply a life lesson to be learned. Relentlessness means never quitting. It means never leaving money on the table, or a solution un tested. Relentless success means constantly thinking about the battle and its process rather than simply achieving a goal. Always developing and refining a system for success will guarantee goal achievement.

As you go beyond the first JAM and into the second JAM session, you must remember the techniques we used to eliminate doubt and focus on forward movement. The following list reminds us of how to defeat doubt and move forward.

11.  Incremental progress everyday 1>0. (Day 13);

12.  The golden rule of three is everywhere, use it to your advantage (Day 4);

13.  Develop and refine your own algorithms (Day 9);

14.  Create an acronym as a reminder of your values (Day 2);

15.  Getting Unstuck (Day 17);

16.  Avoid the nostalgia trap (Day 16);

17.  Defeat Doubt (Day 26);

18.  Use down time wisely (Day 25);

19.  Be in full control of the week by Wednesday (Day 10);

20.  Coming back after a break (Day 24).

As we round out the second JAM session and complete sixty days of productivity we have "learned at least once", and "done at least once", so it's time to "teach others at least once". Use the following tips to get you through the last 10 days.

21.    Learn Once, Do Once, and Teach once (Day 22);

22.    Help Others reach their goals (Day 19);

23.    Believe you can win and help others believe in themselves (Day 21);

24.    Never Seek Pity always seek an advantage (Day 27);

25.    Taking action and making decisions equates to courage (Day 14);

26.    The process is more important than the goals

(Goals v. Process Day 15);

27.    Willpower is a finite resource, rest but always move forward (Day 2);

28.    Realign by focusing on the three pillars Health, Wealth and Wisdom (Day 4);

29.    Reflect and reexamine your JAM journal (day 3);

30.    Dominate the competition (Day 5).

## J.A.M. Journal Writing Cue

List the most important J.A.M. entries from the past thirty days and rank them in accordance with how effective they are. Start the next thirty days with the highest ranked entries and maximize the momentum by starting strong.

## CONCLUSION

There is no formula for success. No book, including this one, is going to give you a blueprint with a step by step fool proof plan for success. But this book will help you develop good habits which will keep you moving forward. The most important thing you can do for yourself is to get started today. Select a goal or dream that you want to accomplish. Deconstruct your goal to smaller steps and try to space it out over thirty days. Each day, apply one of the thirty J.A.M. elements, and execute the incremental tasks which move you towards your final goal. Always remember that the word "Goal" is misleading if there is no system or process associated with it, and the process is infinitely more important than the end result. The J.A.M. is one such process that is reliable and can lead to an ever-increasing progress. Most importantly it is a repeatable system that leads to results.

Journaling is a vital element to success and the J.A.M. expects that you not only keep a journal, but review it. Start your success journal with the writing cues presented in this book and develop and refine your own over time. All successful people keep journals in one form or another. All successful people find the time and we must too.

Create a list of questions to ask yourself in the morning to help you get focused and start writing. I Start thinking about the upcoming weekend as soon as possible. Unlike other people who look forward to meaningless leisure and relaxing, I seek ways to be productive and beat the competition on the weekend. Start your journal by writing down things you will do this weekend. Ask yourself:

What activities worked well and what activities produced the least results?

How many days are left in the JAM and how can I use the remainder to achieve or progress my goals?

How will I end the JAM?

How will I begin the next thirty day cycle with the highest motivation and momentum I can develop?

What marketing ideas will be available today?

What networking opportunities may become available this week?

Can I improve/streamline routine tasks today?

How Can I prepare during the weekend so that on Monday I can engage new products and remain ahead of deadlines?

Are there any new concepts in my concept binder which I can develop into writing articles/lecturers?

What books am I reading this month?

What books do I want to get to this month?

Are there any upcoming opportunities to combine cardio and strength training in my mini vacations?

If I execute the J.A.M. Today how will my life be different in one year from now?

If I do nothing, how will my life change or not change in one year from now?

### <u>Retrospective journaling to identify patterns and triggers.</u>

The goal of J.A.M. is to recognize patterns and triggers that keep you motivated and highly productive. The only way to do that is to reflect and write/record your observations. If I did not keep and review a journal I would never have written this book. This is your life, remember it and record it. Journaling not only releases positive feelings it also improves our memory. If nothing else, keep a journal for the next thirty days and review it often. You will thank me later.

## The January Advantage Method helped me write this book

Prior to writing this guide, I had given a dozen or so lecturers to new entrepreneurs looking to become more productive. I was frequently asked to write a book combining the theories. I usually responded, tongue in cheek, I will, but I have to wait until January to begin. January 1st did not arrive for at least three years.

By writing the thirty steps in thirty days I was self-fulfilling my own theory. I was challenging myself to stay motivated and continue moving forward on the project throughout the month. On January 23, 2016, I had twenty-five pages written and there was a huge snowstorm that walloped the Northeast. I was home-bound. Up until this point I had never made real progress on this project at home. My house was full of distractions, chores and obligations. Up until the snow storm all of my work was done in the office and mostly in cafes.

On the 23rd of January I turned to the book I was writing and implemented one of my rules - "One is greater than zero". I set the most modest goal I could envision "write one sentence today at home". This sentence became one paragraph, then one complete idea then it developed into over an hour of writing in an environment previously untested.

This was my journal entry for that day:

"1/23/15 Today marks the first day that I was able to create content for this project while exclusively at home. I had set a goal of 30 pages in 30 days and missing this day would have set me back. Of course I was locked in due to the blizzard so if I did not write I would have missed my deadline. I set the smallest goal I could think of:

"Write one sentence".

The end result was an impressive hour and half session of writing."

I am certain that I will use the J.A.M. throughout the rest of my life. I will maximize my productive and increase my worth to my business and community. I hope that this method will inspire you to do the same. Thank you and remember to pump up the JAM.

It has been my pleasure and an overwhelming accomplishment for me to write this. IF my work can help just one person get started, get unstuck or get motivated than I have accomplished my goal, thank you dedicated reader.

2016                                   Donald T. Bonomo, Esq.

# RECOMMENDED READING

1. Willpower: rediscovering the greatest human strength,
Roy F. Baumeister- John Tierney Penguin Press 2011

2. Seven Habits Series by Dr. Stephen Covey and the Covey
Institute

3. The Power of Habit: why we do what we do
Charles Duhigg- Random House - 2012

4. Influence: the psychology of persuasion
Robert B. Cialdini- Collins 2007

5. On Writing: a memoir of the craft
Stephen King-Scribner-2000

www.ingramcontent.com/pod-product-compliance
Lightning Source LLC
Chambersburg PA
CBHW070548030426
42337CB00016B/2399